LIVING LANGUAGES
IN CATHOLIC
WORSHIP

LIVING LANGUAGES
IN CATHOLIC
WORSHIP

An Historical Inquiry

by

CYRIL KOROLEVSKY

Priest of the Byzantine rite. Consultant at Rome of the Sacred Eastern Congregation, of the Commission for Eastern Liturgy and of the Commission for the Codification of Eastern Canon Law

Translated by

DONALD ATTWATER

THE NEWMAN PRESS
Westminster Maryland

*First published in France
under the title "Liturgie en Langue
Vivante" by Editions du Cerf: Paris 1955*

This edition first published . . 1957

LIBRARY OF CONGRESS CATALOG CARD NUMBER: 57–11822

PRINTED IN GREAT BRITAIN BY J. AND J. GRAY, EDINBURGH.
NIHIL OBSTAT: HUBERTUS RICHARDS, S.T.L., L.S.S., CENSOR
DEPUTATUS. IMPRIMATUR: E. MORRAGH BERNARD, VIC. GEN.
WESTMONASTERII DIE 2A MAII, 1957

CONTENTS

PART I

THE EAST

PART II

THE WEST

v

CONTENTS

PART III

LATIN INTO DEAD LANGUAGES

PREFACE

THE question of the introduction of some measure of the vernacular or spoken language into the liturgy of worship of the Western or Latin church is a burning one in many countries today, especially among the clergy and members of Catholic Action who are concerned with bringing back to Christ the masses of people who are growing further and further away from Him. . . . .

In 1947 the eleventh issue of *La Maison-Dieu, Cahiers de Pastorale Liturgique*, published in Paris by Éditions du Cerf, was almost entirely devoted to this question. In a very thought-provoking article of nearly fifty pages, called 'Les leçons d'une enquête', Canon A. G. Martimort, professor at the Catholic Institute of Toulouse, discusses the data brought together by the periodical *Témoignage Chrétien* during the autumn of the previous year. Supporters and opponents of the use of Latin are brought face to face in their very outspoken replies. In another article in the same cahier, on 'La discipline de l'Église en matière de langue liturgique', the same writer gives some particulars (pp. 40–45) of the development of this discipline throughout Christendom up to the tenth century. The peoples mentioned are in great part of Eastern rite; and, as Canon Martimort frankly admits, the documentation is not complete.

In the holy year of 1950 there was a great French pilgrimage to Rome to which a large number of parishes sent representatives. Mass was celebrated at midnight in what is left of the old basilica that bears the name of Maxentius, near the Colosseum. I was there, out of sheer curiosity, I must admit. It was what is called a low Mass ('read Mass' would be a better name, as in Italy); and throughout the celebration a speaker—I do not know what else to call him—with the help of a microphone made invocations and gave out objects for prayer at some length: to these the people responded aloud with such acclamations as *Lumen Christi!*: 'The light of Christ!' There seemed to me a parallel between this procedure and our Byzantine *ektenes* or forms of request, rather like the solemn prayers or collects in the Roman liturgy on Good Friday. 'Here', I said to myself, 'is a reaching out towards a new form of liturgy.' Though not fully informed about the details of the problem that had arisen in France and elsewhere, I thought I knew enough about it to venture such a conclusion. It was clear that I was witnessing one of those attempts to enable people to take an active part in public worship without sacrificing the principle of the exclusive use of Latin thereat: a principle which in the opinion of many observers, if not all, is a great difficulty in the way of active participation—perhaps the greatest difficulty.

A careful study of the Cahier I have referred to, and of the then recently published Latin–French Ritual, led me to give further thought to the matter, though it was not one that concerned me directly. And it occurred to me that the testimony of a priest of an Eastern rite about what was and still is done among us, although the position is quite different, could corroborate Canon Martimort's lines of argument and perhaps suggest a solution that it is no business of mine to put forward as definitive. I recalled to mind that, some twenty years before, professional duty and personal interest had required me to examine the question in all its aspects with reference to the Estonian language, and that I had had the happiness of seeing my conclusions adopted.

That is how I came to write this present study. I have purposely omitted any too forbidding scientific apparatus, so as to keep it within the compass of intelligent readers who are, nevertheless, not specialists in ecclesiastical history, Eastern matters and the comparative study of Christian worship. I must make it clear from the start that by peoples of Eastern rite I do not mean only those of the Near East, who after all form only a small minority; I am also looking at the huge masses of Greeks, Rumanians and especially Slavs, nor do I confine myself to Catholics and ignore all our separated brethren. For both, with a few small reservations that I shall not fail to point out, the principles are the same, the historical development is identical and canonical legislation parallel. For the East it is a matter of nearly two hundred million Christians, presumed such in spite of the systematic atheism imposed by communism behind the iron curtain. One day this curtain will be withdrawn—that day may be a long way off yet, but it will come—and it will then be seen that the Christian faith had sent down such deep roots that the atheist campaign, already thirty-five years old, failed to drag them up. Perhaps there will then be so mighty a reaction that the moment will have come to think in practical terms of the union of the churches, or to speak in a way more theologically exact, of the reunion of separated Eastern Christians with the one Church.

This book is divided into two parts. In the first, I deal with the language of public worship in Eastern lands from the beginning of Christianity, explaining the governing principle at work and showing its constant application down to our own time. In the second, I do the same for the West, and show how the Eastern principle, accepted in the West in the ninth century for the apostles of the Slavs, St Cyril and St Methodius, was afterwards restricted in consequence of various circumstances, though never entirely given up; and I carry my inquiry on to the most recent concessions and to current aspirations that still await full approval.[*] I have sometimes been obliged to go into rather lengthy historical details. These are necessary for the proper understanding of how and why legislation developed as it has done; furthermore, the history related is little known, or even not known at all, to most people.

C. K.

Rome,
23 April, 1954

---

[*] The English translator has taken the liberty of arranging two of the author's sections, on a special aspect of his subject, in a separate, third, part.

I

THE EAST

CHAPTER ONE

THE OLDER EASTERN
LITURGICAL LANGUAGES

WHAT was the language of public prayer of the first Christians, those of Palestine in the time of the Apostles? We learn from the book of Acts that, before Gentiles began to be received into the Church, St Peter and St John continued to frequent the Temple, where the Law and the Prophets were read in Hebrew; but the Jews no longer made common use of this language, they spoke Aramaic, which was the tongue in which our Lord Jesus Christ preached.[1] It is certain that the Christian Eucharist, in the short, undeveloped forms of those days, was not celebrated in Hebrew, but in Aramaic. It was the language in which the first of the evangelists, St Matthew, wrote his gospel; but the original text is lost, and only the Greek translation remains.

But from the beginning of St. Paul's journeys and the spread of Christianity in Asia Minor, the situation changed completely. After the conquests of Alexander the Great, the language of communication in those countries which little by little came under Roman control was, not Latin, but Greek; it was spoken in all the urban areas, while the people of the country-side kept their native forms of speech. The whole of the New Testament was written in Greek, even the Epistle to the Romans; Greek was as much spoken in Rome as Latin, and it was the language of the Jewish colony, which there too had adapted itself to its surroundings. The Church in Rome spoke Greek and worshipped in Greek till the middle of the third century, as may be seen from the writings of the oldest Fathers and from ancient monuments. The so-called Apostles' Creed, which was the baptismal symbol of faith at Rome, was

3

originally drawn up in Greek. This spreading of Greek reached
in a measure so far as southern Gaul: in the time of the martyrs
St Pothinus and St Blandina (d. 177), Christians at Lyons, spoke
Greek, and their great bishop St Irenaeus (d. *c.* 203) wrote in it.
(Over a century later, the Emperor Julian wrote only in
Greek.) The native Celtic tongue of the Gauls has left us no
literature, nor has the Punic of North Africa, centred on
Carthage: but there and in Spain, Latin was so widely used
that it seems to have been the language of Christian worship
from the first.

When the barbarians invaded and gradually subdued the
whole of western and central Europe, they were in a primitive
state of linguistic and literary culture, and were quickly
impressed by the prestige of imperial Rome. Greek, which
had never in the West been the tongue of more than a restricted
urban minority, had disappeared, but over wide areas all the
inhabitants who had the smallest claim to education, and many
who had none, spoke Latin, even if it was only Vulgar Latin.
The first written laws of the governing barbarians were drawn
up in that tongue. It is that prestige of Rome and the wide
diffusion of her language, in a form that was already beginning
to change,[2] which accounts for the continued use throughout
so many centuries in the West of Latin for all official acts and
records and for public prayer.

In the East, on the contrary, Latin never took root. After
the Emperor Constantine had removed the imperial capital to
Byzantium, New Rome, Latin continued for a time to be the
language of administration. The Theodosian Code was written
in Latin, so were the Code and Institutes of Justinian. But with
them the sixth century is reached: after Justinian, Greek reigned
supreme at Constantinople for nine hundred years.

Unlike the state of linguistic affairs among the barbarian
peoples of the West, the chief native languages of the East
were already highly developed when Christianity began to
spread widely in the country parts. It was so with Syriac,
almost the whole of whose literature indeed is Christian, but
there are some remains that are not. Coptic was derived from

the language of the ancient Egyptians, which had its own alphabet before adopting that of the Greeks, and was already divided into five dialects. Armenian was in use for public affairs and records before Armenia's conversion to Christianity; it was the difficulty of expressing all the sounds of this language with the Greek alphabet that led to the invention of the Armenian alphabet.

The Emergence of Rites

In those far-off days, the end of the third and the beginning of the fourth century, the Christian liturgy of public worship was not yet fixed. It was slowly elaborating in the great centres, and developing into what nowadays are called 'rites': a Roman rite at Rome, Ambrosian at Milan, Gallican in Gaul, Celtic in parts of Britain and in Ireland, Mozarabic in Spain, all in Latin. In the East, the Alexandrian rite soon appears at Alexandria, the Antiochene in Syria and in a measure in Mesopotamia and Persia, and, a little later, the Armenian in Armenia. Lesser churches followed the examples of those in the more important cities, until formulas were reached which became fixed, or very nearly so: these borrowed from one another, and sometimes combinations were effected. Thus the Byzantine rite of today (often improperly called the Greek rite) is derived from the Alexandrian and the Antiochene; the rite of the modern Chaldeans and of the Nestorians of Mesopotamia and the mountains of Kurdistan is more autonomous, but it is connected with Edessa, which was a great centre of learning for eastern Syria; the Alexandrian rite, mixed with Syrian elements in accordance with the nationality of missionaries, spread to Ethiopia; the Armenian rite is a mixture of old Byzantine and Antiochene, completed by its own contributions.

And so we get the five Eastern rites that subsist to this day: the Antiochene or West Syrian; the Persian or East Syrian, which since the sixteenth century has been called Chaldean by the West; the Alexandrian, sometimes improperly called

Coptic, with its Ethiopian branch; the Armenian; and lastly the Byzantine.[3] This last, thanks to the work of missionaries, was destined to have a quite special diffusion; those who use it today form far and away the greater part of those Christians of various communions who make up the Eastern churches, often inaccurately referred to as the 'Greek Church'.

In the West, almost all rites and variants gradually yielded to that of Rome, the immediate metropolis. The Ambrosian rite is still observed in Milan and in parts of some neighbouring dioceses; but the Mozarabic is used in only a single chapel, at Toledo, the Gallican disappeared in the age of Charlemagne, and the Celtic liturgy did not survive much longer. There also remain today more or less extensive variant observances and texts used by certain dioceses and religious orders: the Carthusians, the Dominicans, whose ceremonial is considerably different from the current Roman, the Carmelites of the Old Observance, who have kept the rite of the Latin patriarchate of Jerusalem at the time of the Crusades; the usages of the archdiocese of Lyons and of the Portuguese archdiocese of Braga.[4]

The Use of National Languages in the East

At the time when the different rites began to be fixed, a curious and characteristic phenomenon is to be observed: the whole of the West kept to the Latin language, but in the East national tongues were everywhere used.

It used to be said quite confidently that this was due to the heresies of the first eight centuries, which mostly originated in the East, and died there, except for two that still subsist. Even the distinguished Dom Guéranger upheld this simple-minded opinion; but nobody believes it today. Nor is the attribution of the liturgical use of national languages to political considerations in any better case.

Syria, for example, was discontented with the Byzantine régime, and accordingly welcomed the Arab invasion of 636; but the Syrians who did this included the Greek-speakers as well as the Syriac-speakers. At first only foreigners left the country, the more so as its new rulers, the Omayyad khalifs, began by being tolerant. It was only with the coming of the Abbasid khalifs of Baghdad, after 750, that the persecution of Christians, sporadic until then, was intensified through the perpetual state of war between the Arabs and the emperor at Constantinople. Then an exodus of hellenized Syrians did begin, while those of Syriac speech, who were less obnoxious to the government, stayed where they were. During the tenth century, the Byzantines returned to Syria for a time, and pushed on to the gates of Jerusalem. Those of the Syrians who had not succumbed to the monophysite or monothelite heresies gradually adopted the Byzantine rite, but translating it from Greek into Syriac; this use of Syriac among them persisted till the sixteenth century, and in some places into the seventeenth, when it was replaced by Arabic, which everybody was speaking by that time. Or again in Egypt, where the Bible was read in church in Coptic from the second half of the third century; at that time there was not yet any question of monophysite heresy or of reaction against Byzantine domination. To this day the Copts keep whole passages of their liturgy in Greek.

The real reason why national tongues have continued to be used in Christian worship is because there was no reason for not using them, but rather the contrary.

Wherever they penetrated, the first care of missionaries was to translate the Bible into the language of the country in which they found themselves, beginning with the gospels and the rest of the New Testament. The Syriac version of the Bible goes back to the end of the second century; the Coptic version, in three different dialects, to the third; the Armenian version to the fourth. Karthvelia or Georgia, south of the Caucasus, was evangelized from the fourth century by Greeks, and the translation of at least the four gospels dates from the end of that century or the beginning of the next. When the essential biblical books had been translated, the same was done for the liturgical offices that the missionaries brought with them.

Eastern Liturgical Languages to the Twelfth Century

Eastern liturgical languages are numerous. Apart from Greek, there were seven up to the twelfth century, the time at which the principle of their use was authoritatively formulated. Since then, more still have come into use, but for the moment I am concerned only with the first seven.

I have no intention here of offering a course in linguistics or lexicography. My aim is simply to enumerate the languages, noting who uses them and in what measure, with some relevant statistics. It is, however, impossible to make oneself understood without clarifying the meaning of certain terms that are often misunderstood or to which a wrong signification is often given.

The first of these languages is *Syriac*, a Semitic tongue divided into two branches; these are not differentiated by grammar and vocabulary, which are identical, but by the system of writing and pronunciation: they are Western Syriac and Eastern Syriac. In the sixteenth century, the second of these was dubbed Chaldean in Europe, although it is no more than related to the ancient speech of Chaldea. In its classical form and in the form called Aramaic (referred to at the beginning of this chapter), Syriac was diffused throughout Syria, except in the great centres of hellenization, and in Palestine and Mesopotamia. It ceased to be spoken at the end of the middle ages; but it has survived in a modified form in two or three villages of the Damascus plain and among many of the Christians of Iraq, where it is called Sureth. The first stages of the Antiochene or West Syrian rite were in Greek, later translated into Syriac; but the Chaldean or East Syrian rite has always been in Syriac.

Syriac continues to be the language of worship among the following: the Nestorians of Kurdistan, now reduced to a few tens of thousands of souls; the Catholic Chaldeans (numbering some 125,000); the monophysite Syrians or 'Jacobites' (about 150,000 in Syria and Iraq); the Catholic (West) Syrians (80,000); the Maronites of the Lebanon, all Catholics and numbering some 500,000, including those in the Americas; and in India by the Catholic Malabarese (1,100,000), the Catholic Malankarese (80,000), the Malabar Jacobites (600,000), and a few Nestorians: altogether, some two and three-quarter million Christians of all the relevant ecclesiastical allegiances. The Melkites of Syria (see below, under Arabic) used Syriac concurrently with Greek until the seventeenth century.

The second language is *Coptic*, the last stage in the evolution of the ancient Egyptian tongue. It has not been spoken since the seventeenth century, and its sole use now is in the liturgy of Christians of the Alexandrian rite. Of these, at least a million are monophysite dissidents and about 65,000 Catholics. The Copts are found only in Egypt.

The third language is *Armenian*, an Indo-European tongue spoken only by the people of that name. Their homeland is south of the Caucasus, where they form the Soviet republic of Armenia or Hayastan. They were nearly as numerous in the former Ottoman empire, where they formed a large element in the population of several vilayets or provinces in Asia Minor; here they were dispersed by the successive massacres for which the responsibility fell on the Sultan Abd ul-Hamid and on the Young Turks. The Armenians are exceedingly able business-men, very attached to their nationality and their language, and they are found all over the Near East, in Europe and America, and so far away as India and the East Indian islands. Their number is difficult to estimate: one might hazard a total of five million, most of them monophysite Christians, with perhaps 150,000 Catholics of their rite and some thousands of Protest-ants. Armenian takes two forms: the old classical language, which is only used in the liturgy, to the exclusion of all other; and modern Armenian, which is not greatly different from the classical.

The fourth language is *Georgian*, also called Karthvelian or Iberian. It is a very ancient speech and, like Basque in Spain and France, its origin is unknown. In ethnic type the Georgians are Indo-European, but that is all that can be said. They live

south of the Caucasus, north of Armenia, where they have
been organized into the Soviet republic of Sakartvelo, largely
made up of the former governorate of Tiflis (Tbilisi). The
Georgians number over two million, all Christians of the
dissident Orthodox Church, except for a few thousand
Catholics. These last follow the Armenian or the Latin rite;
they are in danger of disappearance for lack of a bishop, and
therefore, in due course, of priests. The Georgian language has
undergone but little evolution through the ages and it remains
much the same as it was in its classical era, from the tenth to the
thirteenth centuries. The Byzantine liturgy was translated into
it gradually, at an uncertain epoch; the process was finished
perhaps in the eleventh century. Before that, Syriac and
Armenian, and probably Greek, were used.

The fifth language is *Ge'ez* which, like Hebrew, Syriac and
Arabic, is a Semitic tongue. It was at one time spoken in
Ethiopia, undergoing a gradual transformation in the course of
centuries, under the influence of the speech of Amhara (the
region round Gondar) and of African dialects. Ge'ez is still
the exclusive language of the Ethiopic liturgy; but in civil
affairs it has been superseded by Amharic, though without
prejudice to a number of local dialects. Amharic is now the
official language of Ethiopia (Abyssinia); it is Semitic-Hamitic,
and includes many words from Ge'ez. Apart from its use in
public worship, Ge'ez to-day is no more than an 'accomplish-
ment', understood only by people of some learning.

Ethiopia became Christian from the middle of the fourth
century onwards, being evangelized by missionaries from
Egypt and Syria. It was through this contact with countries
where Monophysism came to predominate that the Ethiopian
Christians were insensibly drawn into that heresy; their one
bishop was appointed by the monophysite Coptic patriarch at
Alexandria. Their liturgy, as has already been noted, is
substantially that of the Copts, modified by local features; its
translation into Ge'ez was partly through the medium of
Arabic. Such is the mixture of races and religions (Islam,
Judaism, heathenism) that the Christian population of Ethiopia

is difficult to ascertain; it is perhaps three million, of whom 60,000 are Catholics of Ethiopic rite.

The sixth language is *Staroslav* or *Paleoslav*, Old Slavonic, often referred to as Church Slavonic. It is now a dead language, but it was very much alive in the eighth century and was more or less common to all the Slav tribes, whose territory extended as far west as the Elbe; it was only during the ninth century that their dialects began to diverge. Since that era, the events of history have dislocated the Slavonic world: the Slavs of the south have been cut off from those of the north, and those of the west have turned in a different direction from those of the east. In spite of its close relationship to Russian, Staroslav is not the mother of Russian, but rather its sister; and it owes its fame to the fact that into it were translated the Bible, the Byzantine liturgical books, and also those of Rome. The Poles soon disciplined their language and for long made extensive use of Latin in public affairs; but for the rest of the Slavs, until the sixteenth century, Staroslav was what Latin was for the West— the language of educated people and scholars.

Apart from the small body of 'Glagolites', who will be mentioned later on, Staroslav is the liturgical language of Slavs of Byzantine rite: Russians proper, Byelorussians, Ukrainians or Ruthenians,[5] Serbs and Bulgars; the last two peoples are isolated by their geographical position, being separated from the rest by the Hungarians and Rumanians. An over-all total of numbers is rather speculative: say a hundred million Russians, perhaps ten million Byelorussians (a small part of whom are of Latin rite), forty million Ukrainians, over six million Serbs, and rather fewer Bulgars: in all, about a hundred and sixty million. It may be said that the Christians of Byzantine rite, so often miscalled 'the Greek Church', are numerically above all a 'Slav church'. The liturgical texts are, with little variation, the same everywhere, and differences of pronunciation of Staroslav are slight.

As for the ecclesiastical allegiances of this vast mass of people, before the violent suppressions by the Soviet government one could reckon six million Catholics as against some hundred and fifty-five million dissident Orthodox of various obediences. Those who have in recent years been forcibly aggregated to the Orthodox Church continue to resist passively, awaiting an opportunity to renew their allegiance to Rome. As the result of voluntary emigration that began in the nineteenth century, followed by the upheavals of two world wars, there are now many Slav Orthodox and Slav-Byzantine Catholics dispersed in various parts of Europe and elsewhere, and they are found in more compact bodies in the Americas. The United States and Canada alone have nearly a million such Catholics.

The seventh and last living tongue adopted by Eastern liturgies before the twelfth century is *Arabic*. The wide diffusion of this language followed the Muslim conquests, which absorbed all the peoples who spoke Syriac and Coptic and in part those who spoke Greek. Arabic begins to appear in public worship from the tenth century, first for the biblical readings and the rubrics, then in varying degrees for the other parts. To-day the Melkite[6] Catholics and Orthodox in Syria, Palestine and Egypt have all their liturgical books in Arabic; there are a few phrases in Greek, always permissive, but the people would not tolerate any service celebrated wholly or mostly in Greek. They number at least 200,000 Catholics in the above countries and America, and some 400,000 Orthodox in the same regions.

The Coptic liturgical books are all bilingual or in Arabic alone, and Arabic is extensively used. The Chaldeans are faithful to their Syriac, but the eucharistic epistle and gospel are often read only in Arabic. The Maronites keep the whole of the Office, properly so called, in Syriac; but a notable part of the eucharistic Liturgy and of the other sacramental rites is in Arabic, as are all 'devotions' of modern origin, which are numerous among them. This Arabic is printed in their liturgical books in Syriac characters, an arrangement that is called Karshuni. It is the same with the (West) Syrian Catholics and Jacobites, but among them the use of Arabic is more limited. Among the Indians of West Syrian rite the place of

Arabic is taken by the local Malayalam, of which an account will be given later.

Local Practices in the Far East

It is possible, but not certain, that some Nestorian Christians used to have liturgical prayers and hymns in Persian as well as in Syriac.[7] This Persian was the language called Pahlavi, a derivative from the ancient tongue of the Achemenids and a stage towards modern Persian. It also seems possible that they translated parts of their liturgy into Chinese,[8] and the thirteenth-century traveller William of Rubruck provides evidence for Uigur Turkish. He says: 'We came across one large town there [in eastern Kazakhstan] called Cailac. . . . That country used to be called Organum and used to have its own language and script. . . . Also the Nestorians of those parts used to perform their services and write books in that script and language.' Later on Friar William says: 'There are Nestorians in fifteen cities of Cathay and they have a bishopric there. . . . [The Nestorians] say their offices and have their sacred books in Syriac, a language of which they are ignorant, and so they sing like our monks who know no grammar, and this accounts for the fact that they are completely corrupt.'[9] This shows that the Uigur Turkish version had only a restricted use.

There is a document that gives other interesting particulars about these Turkish Christians. Its editor, Alphonse Mingana, thinks it may have been composed at Baghdad between 730 and 790, by a Syrian Jacobite writer, and the manuscript itself dates from about 1040. Mingana suggests that the writer's information may have come from a Turkish deputation waiting upon the Nestorian katholikos[10] for the ordination of a metropolitan for their own country. The following passage occurs in this document:

They [the Christian Turks] do not learn nor do they accept any other script besides our own, and in the language of us Syrians they write and read the books of the two Testaments, the Old and the New, and the writings of the orthodox Fathers. In

their gatherings they translate the above books into their Turkish
language, while they never venture to change into the Turkish
language the adorable name of our divine Lord Jesus Christ nor
that of Mary, the mother of God,[11] but they pronounce them
as they are in our Syriac language. As to the rest of the words
and names they render them into the Turkish language, in order
that all their congregation may understand what is read.[12]

The fact is that we now know that Christianity had penetrated into Turkish territory through Khorasan and the marches
of Transoxiana from the fourth century, or even the third. A
bishop at Merv in Khorasan is recorded in 334, and by 420 that
town was a metropolitan see. At the beginning of the ninth
century the Katholikos Timothy I sent missionaries to Kara-
korum, south of Lake Baikal, and Bar-Hebraeus (d. 1286)
alleges that, around the year 1000, Kerait Turks were being
baptized by hundreds of thousands in the depths of the Gobi
desert. The history of these Turkish Christians can be followed
down to the end of the thirteenth century.

Thus we see applied in the far parts of Asia the same principle
of translation that the late fourth-century Spanish pilgrim,
Etheria, recorded of the mixed-language Christians of Palestine;
there, she tells us, what was read in Greek was immediately
repeated in Syriac for the benefit of those who did not know
Greek. It is exactly the practice of contemporary international
conferences—without the aids provided by modern technique!

Formulation of the Eastern Principle

The seven, with Greek, eight, languages just enumerated are
far from being the only ones used in Eastern liturgies. But,
before going on to more modern tongues, we must pause to
examine the declaration of principle in the matter made by
Theodore Balsamon in reply to a question put to him by a
Melkite patriarch, Mark of Alexandria.[13] Balsamon, himself
a pure Byzantine, was the greatest of Byzantine canonists; he
was patriarch of Antioch between 1185 and 1195, but in consequence of the opposition to him of the occupying Crusaders

he went to live at Constantinople. His writings, a series of more or less detailed commentaries on every part of conciliar and patristic law, were received (unlike the politico-religious decrees of the emperors) into the official body of ancient canon law of all the Byzantine churches, and they are authoritative. His replies to the sixty-four questions of Mark of Alexandria were not incorporated in the same way; but they share the authority of his other works and are often appealed to.

The fifth of Mark's questions was concerned with Syrian and Armenian priests in Egypt who had not fallen into the heresy of Monophysism. Should they be allowed to go on celebrating the holy Mysteries in their own language, or should they be required to celebrate in Greek? Balsamon rested his reply on St Paul's words to the Romans (3: 29): 'Is God the God of the Jews only, and not of the Gentiles also? Indeed of the Gentiles also.' And he concluded that: 'Those who are wholly orthodox, but who are altogether ignorant of the Greek tongue, shall celebrate in their own language; provided only that they have exact versions of the customary prayers, translated [literally, "copied"] on to rolls and well written in Greek characters.'

All that Balsamon requires is that the translation should be exact. He does not refer to any approval of the version; but clearly control is needed, and equally clearly it should be exercised by the hierarchical authority or his delegate. When we come to Pope John VIII approving the use of Slavonic in 879, he will not refer to control either; but he was dealing with the work of St Methodius, head of the Moravian mission, and at that era it was not considered necessary to be more precise. In due course Pope Pius XI will lay it down that the approval of every new language pertains to the Apostolic See.

The Use of Rumanian

An important Eastern liturgical language, but one not introduced till much later, is *Rumanian*.

The origins of the Rumanian people are very obscure. They

are traditionally regarded as descendants of the Roman
colonists whom the Emperor Trajan planted in Dacia. However that may be, it is unquestionable that the Rumanians are
of Latin stock.[14] Their anthropological type suggests it, and
their language is neo-Latin: three quarters of its words are
popular Latin slightly modified, and the rest are borrowings
from different peoples with whom they have been in contact.
Their first evangelizers were Latins; with some likelihood
they claim as their apostle St Nicetas of Remesiana (d. *c.* 414),[15]
who may have been the author of the thanksgiving hymn,
Te Deum. Their original liturgy will then have been of
Western type.

But during the high middle ages the Rumanians formed part
of the Bulgarian empire, whose civil and ecclesiastical language
was Slavonic, and with the language came the rite. Accordingly, the Rumanians have for many centuries been of Byzantine
rite. Their clergy celebrated in Staroslav up to the time when
Slavonic culture, represented by the monastic element, ceased
to be able to maintain itself in Rumanian lands; the editions
produced at Targoviste and Brasov are among the oldest
typographical records of the Byzantine liturgy in Staroslav.
After Constantinople fell to the Turks in 1453, many Greek
monks fled for refuge among the Rumanians, and so introduced another cultural element. Deprived of the support of
the Bulgarian empire, which had been broken up by the Turks,
Slavonic culture declined more and more; the lower clergy
were still able to read Staroslav but could no longer understand it, and they had neither the wish nor the opportunity to
learn it.

During the latter part of the fifteenth century, whether under
the influence of the Hussites or of the great Moldavian monasteries, or of both, the Psalms, the Acts and Epistles, and
probably the Gospels, were translated into Rumanian. This
was perhaps done for liturgical use, but it is difficult to be sure,
for the translation is known only from manuscripts that are
defective or now lost; from a linguistic point of view, these
manuscripts are not wholly in agreement with the sixteenth-

century printed versions, which were all made for use in divine worship.[16]

During the second half of the sixteenth century, Protestantism was introduced among the Saxons of Transylvania, and it was soon adopted also by considerable numbers of Hungarians. These having the mastery, they did all they could to induce the Rumanians there to follow their example, and were willing to use force when required. In 1564 there was a schism among the Protestants: the Saxons remained Lutheran, while the Hungarians became Calvinist. A Calvinist church was organized, which kept the exterior framework and titles of the Orthodox hierarchy, and catechisms were printed by both Saxons and Hungarians. Although these catechisms certainly existed, not a single copy of any one of them has survived. In 1571 a Catholic prince came to the throne of Transylvania, Stephen Bathori, who was afterwards king of Poland. In the following year he gave a special bishop to the Transylvanian Rumanians who had not become Protestant, and appointed them a second bishop in 1574. There continued to be a Calvinist superintendent or bishop, but his campaign came to an end: although they were serfs of the Hungarian gentry, the Rumanian peasants were not much touched by Protestantism.

Still, it was a very dangerous situation and the Rumanian bishops realized it. Their priests were incapable of preaching; but there was still the liturgy, which is a real education in itself, provided that the people understand it. This the Rumanians could not do in Slavonic. So perhaps the existing Rumanian versions of psalms, epistles and gospels were brought into use; in any case translation of the liturgical books was put in hand, and one by one they were printed. The Gospel book was published in 1561, the Acts and Epistles (*Apostol*) in 1563, the Psalter in 1570, the three eucharistic Liturgies in 1683, the *Horologion*, or ordinary of the Divine Office, and the Deacon's book in 1687, the *Eukhologion* or Ritual in 1689; this last was to replace the edition of 1564, which was more Calvinist than Orthodox. There is no point in continuing the list.

In the course of the years 1696–1700 a large proportion of

B

the Rumanians in Transylvania came into union with the Holy See; thereupon young men went to study in Rome, and afterwards took a big part in the development of Rumanian literature. A printing-works was set up at Blaj and began to produce little books of religious instruction; from 1757–60 it undertook the printing of service-books as well. This press continued to be active until the communist government violently suppressed the Rumanian Catholics of Byzantine rite in 1948. At that date there were some ten million Orthodox in Rumania, and about one and a half million Byzantine Catholics, nearly all in Transylvania (Ardeal).

Until the middle of the nineteenth century the Rumanian language was printed in Cyrillic characters, the last remaining vestige of Slavonic culture. A transition was then undertaken to Roman characters, which are much more suited to the genius of the language, and to-day they are everywhere in exclusive use.[17] No modification of the Roman alphabet was required, apart from diacritical marks to indicate particular pronunciations of *a*, *s*, and *t*.

The Attitude of the Holy See

When considering liturgical languages in the East, it is important to notice that for nineteen hundred years Rome seems never to have given any attention to the matter. It was well known that the East used a number of languages in public worship; so well known that several references were made to the fact at the Council of Trent, when the Western liturgical language was under discussion. But there is no trace whatever of any Roman intervention in the East under this head, whether to allow or disallow, to approve or disapprove. The fact of the use of various languages was there, and it was simply accepted.

The Maronites of the Lebanon had been drawn into an acceptance of Monothelism, which they believed in complete good faith to be orthodox doctrine. When they came to recognize their mistake at the time of the Crusades, Pope

Innocent III tried to impose certain Western usages on them; but he did not say a word about their language of worship. Nor was anything said of this matter during the various negotiations associated with the Council of Florence in 1439, when unity was momentarily restored among Christians. Nor, again, was it raised in 1552, when the Nestorian katholikos, John Sulaqa, came to Rome to re-establish the long-broken hierarchical communion of his people. Clement VIII made not the least objection to the use of Slavonic by the Ruthenians after the Union of Brest in 1595, nor did Innocent XII or Clement XI in respect of Rumanian at the Transylvanian union of 1696–1700.

There was certainly formal intervention by Rome in the ninth century, when Pope John VIII recognized the legitimacy of using the Slavonic tongue; but here, as we shall see, it was a question of translating Roman formularies, not Byzantine. Moreover, we shall also see that Rome looked with a favourable eye on the translation of certain of her books into Croat and Albanian, and that Urban VIII had the same breadth of view in regard to Persian and Slavonic.

Restrictive Legislation by Catholic Synods

A first example of a somewhat different attitude is furnished by the Maronite Synod of the Lebanon in 1736, for which the preparatory work was done in Rome by the famous Joseph Simon Assemani,[18] undoubtedly with the help of Roman canonists. The synod's treatment of the question of liturgical language seems to derogate a little from the Eastern principle that the use of any tongue is permissible, provided the translation be faithful. The pertinent passages of the synodical acts begin by rehearsing, sometimes word for word, the well-known dispositions of the Council of Trent on the matter. They then 'allow and concede' the maintenance of the age-long and universal usage of all Eastern Christian communities, of singing and saying certain parts of divine worship in the spoken tongue, Arabic in this case. Certain conditions,

however, are laid down: the use of Syriac must be retained and
often employed; the bilingual text, in two columns, Syriac
and Arabic, must appear in all books, whether manuscript or
printed; the translation must be examined and approved by the
patriarch; and it is forbidden to translate extempore while
actually celebrating an office. In more solemn celebrations of
the eucharistic Liturgy, the epistle and gospel must be read or
sung in Syriac first, before being given in Arabic. The passage
concludes by repeating the anathema, in the words of the
canon of the Council of Trent, against those who maintain
that Mass must everywhere be celebrated in the spoken
tongue. These prescriptions are observed by the Maronites
today.

Western influence was obviously at work, and this synod,
whose acts were approved by Pope Benedict XIV *in forma
specifica*, has been influential on a number of points in subsequent Catholic councils in the Near East. This influence has
been the stronger because of general ignorance of the true
Eastern discipline and because of the extensive use of manuals
of Western canon law.

Thus we find that the synod of the (West) Syrian Catholics,
held at Sharfeh in the Lebanon in 1888, laid down precise rules
as to what must be said or sung in Syriac and what may be in
Arabic. It rejected the custom among the dissident Jacobites
of translating liturgical texts into other languages, such as
Turkish and Kurdish; and it strongly condemned the practice
of extempore translation. This last prohibition was regarded
as so important that it was referred to twice: it was certainly
thoroughly justified.[19] Though the passages allowed in Arabic
are fairly numerous, and in accordance with recognized
custom, one cannot but notice a certain suggestion of restriction. This is partly due to the influence of the Western
principle of 'Latin only'; but it also owes something to the
high regard that both West and East Syrians have for their
ancient tongue, which, as has already been pointed out, is still
spoken in a modified form in some regions. On three days of
the year, only Syriac may be used in the liturgy: namely, on

Christmas eve, Easter eve, and St Ephrem's day (which with them is the first Saturday in Lent).

The Syrian Mass-book published by the Congregation for the Spreading of the Faith (*de Propaganda Fide*) in 1843 contained a number of short passages in Arabic, printed in Syriac characters (Karshuni), and all the general rubrics were in Arabic only. The revised edition issued by the Patriarch Ephrem II Rahmani in 1922 is of a similar character. The epistle and gospel are generally read in Arabic alone, but in both languages on solemnities. The Ritual published by the Patriarch George Shelhot at Beirut in 1872 contained much Arabic, printed in its proper characters; Ephrem II's revision (Sharfeh, 1922) restored Karshuni for this. All the other service-books are wholly in Syriac.

The Coptic synod held at Cairo in 1898 was influenced more by the Synod of Sharfeh than by that of the Maronites. No more than one short paragraph is given to the language of public worship. This simply says that, though Coptic and Greek have not been currently spoken for a long time, it is nevertheless not allowable for priests and other sacred ministers to use the spoken tongue at will in divine worship.[20] That is all. In practice, however, there is a tendency among the Catholics, as well as among the dissidents, more and more to substitute Arabic for Coptic, even though the latter is now better taught than it used to be; ignorance of a language that has been completely dead since the seventeenth century has not been without serious disadvantages in the ministration of the sacraments—baptism, for example.[21]

A plenary council of the Armenians was held in Rome in 1911, and this devoted five canons to the matter of liturgical language.[22] As was to be expected, they were distinctly Western in tendency. The language of public worship is classical Armenian; the gospel at Mass may be read a second time, in modern Armenian or any other tongue; but this second reading must not be done with the ceremony that accompanies the first. Living languages are forbidden in certain rites borrowed from the West, such as Benediction of the Blessed Sacrament.[23] On the other hand, spoken tongues are allowed for various 'devotions', also borrowed from the West (Analogous observances of the East normally take a liturgical form). All the services in question must be examined and approved by the local bishop. Taken all in all, these canons simply reproduce the legislation of the Western church.

In face of these prescriptions the Armenian Catholics of Aleppo, who have spoken nothing but Arabic for at least two hundred years, are anxious for the introduction of that language, which they hear used so much in the churches of their Melkite, Maronite and Syrian neighbours. This has been done for baptisms and weddings. But the bishops are opposed to it, because it would take away yet a little more from the national character: everybody knows how attached the Armenians are to their nationality, language and customs. Nevertheless, this movement is likely to spread to Beirut and the Lebanon, where Armenians are very numerous since the massacres and great exodus of the first World War; and it will be very difficult to continue to resist it.

In pre-1945 Poland the state of affairs was even worse. Before the Soviet government destroyed it, there was an Armenian diocese centred on Lvov, which numbered five thousand or so faithful there and in parts of Bucovina. Among these people the eucharistic Liturgy, very westernized, was still celebrated in classical Armenian, but in a low voice; and during it the congregation sang hymns in Polish to Polish airs. Then there was the Armenian colony at Gherla in Transylvania and its other four parishes, in a district whose language was largely Hungarian. I have in my possession a copy of a hymn-book that they used. It gives on one page the text of the hymns in the Armenian language and characters, and on the opposite page the transcription into Roman characters according to Hungarian phonetics. The ecclesiastical organization of these people, numbering some thirty-five thousand souls, has also been destroyed by the communist government.

CHAPTER TWO

THE HUNGARIAN LANGUAGE

A NY restriction on the use of a living tongue in Eastern
worship did not emanate from Rome itself until 1896,
and then it was a matter of Hungarian (Magyar).
Nevertheless, although the prohibition of this language was
repeated several times, it has remained inoperative in practice,
and it has not been renewed since 1922. The fact remains that
Hungarian was forbidden, contrary to the Eastern principle,
and the prohibition is still theoretically in force: the reason for
this was a concatenation of very complex factors which must
now be explained. A good deal of detail is necessary, because
the matter is entirely unknown outside the circles concerned,
and within those circles it has never been treated in a way that
is free from the influence of the worst of all passions where
religion is concerned—political passion. The present writer is
neither Hungarian nor Rumanian; but he has the advantage
of having stayed long enough in Hungary and in Rumania
to be able to give an account that is first-hand and, he hopes,
impartial.[1]

The northern part of Hungary proper and the west of
Transylvania comprise certain bodies of Catholics of Byzantine
rite, often compact, together with a small minority of dissident
Orthodox. Before the first World War, they belonged to the
five eparchies or dioceses[2] of Eperies (in Slav, Preshov) and
Munkacs (Mukachevo), which are Ruthenian, Nagyvarad (in
Rumanian, Oradea Mare), Szamos-Ujvar (Gherla) and
Balaszfalva (Blaj), which are Rumanian. In everyday life,
these people speak Hungarian or Podcarpathian Ruthenian or
Rumanian; but many of them, especially among the better
educated, are bilingual, knowing Ruthenian and Hungarian or

Rumanian and Hungarian. The respective numbers are impossible to ascertain accurately, because of the very irregular distribution of the languages, but even more because of political propaganda. It is rather like Macedonia, where the people are, or call themselves, Greeks, Bulgars or Serbs; or Alsace, where everybody is French by nationality and feeling, but some speak only Alsatian, others only French, while the majority understand and speak both. If one must give a figure, those who speak only Hungarian may be a quarter-million, and at least as many are more or less bilingual. It is impossible even to make a guess at how many use Ruthenian alone or Rumanian alone.

Those who are of Ruthenian origin began to come through the Carpathian passes from the Western Ukraine during the fourteenth century; those of Rumanian origin have come down gradually from the eastern Carpathians and the Transylvanian Alps in the course of centuries. Their ecclesiastical communion with Rome dates from the second half of the seventeenth century.

It takes several generations for a people to change its language, but in these regions, as elsewhere, it happened; and this in spite of the great differences of structure and vocabulary between the Indo-European tongues, Ruthenian and Rumanian, and the Uralian Hungarian, which is related to Finnish, Estonian and dialects of northern Siberia. Little by little some of the immigrants who had settled down, and were not simply migrant workers at harvest-time and so on, forgot their own tongue and found themselves speaking Hungarian, especially those who lived nearer to the middle of the great plain of Hungary.

The first translations seem to have been made in the seventeenth century. According to oral tradition, the first pieces translated were the twelve 'passion gospels' read in the evening of Holy Thursday, the long prayers at Vespers of Pentecost, the blessing of the waters at Epiphany, and the prayers for the ministering of the sacraments. Then came the turn of the three eucharistic Liturgies,[3] beginning with that of St John

Chrysostom, which was printed in Hungarian at Ungvar (Uzhorod) in 1795; but the translation existed in manuscript long before that, together with many of the chants of Vespers and Matins. The people with whom we are concerned are very religious and passionately fond of singing in church. The sexes are separated, the women in galleries, the men massed in the nave, and all respond in chorus to the officiating priest. I have often been present at their services: it is a striking experience.

In 1825 a collection of chants in Hungarian appeared at Kassa (Kosice) in Slovakia, and another at Debreczen in 1862. No music was printed with them; the very simple melodies, inspired by the Slav chant, were known by heart and passed on from mouth to mouth. These collections were officially approved in 1863 by the bishop of Munkacs, Basil Popovich, who at the same time warned against the use of Hungarian in the eucharistic Liturgy until the translation had been carefully examined and authorized. The bishop did not say which authority would do this; but he had already been delated to the Hungarian primate, and no doubt he wished to avoid further complications; he must have known perfectly well that the Hungarian version had been in use for a long time. Fundamentally, its use was simply an application of the pertinent Eastern principle; and nothing would have been said about it had it not been for the explosion of Hungarian nationalism after 1848, and especially after the battle of Sadova in 1866.[4]

North-west of Debreczen in the Hungarian plain there is a considerable town called Hajdudorog, whose population is almost entirely composed of Catholics of Byzantine rite. Here in 1868 there was held a conference representing some fifty parishes. Its object was to elect a committee of clergy and laity which was to open negotiations with the Austro-Hungarian sovereign, the royal chancellery, the parliament and the Hungarian primate for the organization of a diocese distinct from the neighbouring Ruthenian and Rumanian dioceses. The moving spirit in this enterprise was Lewis Farkas, a lawyer belonging to the chief landowning family of the place. In due course, in 1873, a royal decree went a long way towards meeting this request, by making Hajdudorog an episcopal vicariate for what it called 'the Greek-Catholic Hungarians';[5] and the bishop of Munkacs, Stephen Pankovich, proceeded to the nomination of the first incumbent. A commission of nine members of the clergy of the Ruthenian dioceses, Munkacs and Eperies, was entrusted with the revision of the liturgical translations, and their work was finished in 1879. During the following three years, five volumes were published, covering the essential requirements of the pastoral liturgy. It is the opinion of all who have examined them that these Hungarian versions, made from the Staroslav of the Ruthenian books, are faithful and exact.

The organization set up in 1873 functioned without mis-adventure for twenty-three years. In their periodical reports to the Congregation for the Spreading of the Faith, the Ruthenians and Rumanian bishops said nothing about any movement among some of their faithful in favour of using Hungarian in church services; to oppose this language was precisely further to excite a nationalist temper that Rome had no intention of encouraging. Not in origin, but in present fact, the people around Hajdudorog felt and called themselves Hungarian; by using the relevant tongue in worship they were simply applying the principle always recognized in the Eastern churches, and they had followed this practice for some two centuries without anyone ever thinking of questioning it.

And no one did question it until 1896. On 27 June in that year, on the occasion of the millenary celebrations of the kingdom of Hungary, the episcopal vicar of Hajdudorog celebrated a solemn Liturgy[6] in Hungarian in the university church at Budapest. This was duly reported in the newspapers, among them the *Pester Lloyd* of Budapest, which was one of the papers regularly read in the secretariate of state at the Vatican. This time Rome was moved to act. Information was asked for, and the Latin-rite bishop of Szekesfehervar, Philip Steiner, sent a report that aroused lively interest. Mgr Steiner was not

altogether wrong when he attributed the movement for a
purely Hungarian diocese of Eastern rite to nationalism and
liberalism, nor when he gave the impression that it would lead
to a demand for the liturgy in their own tongue among the
Hungarians of Latin rite. This was all part of the truth; but
there was unquestionably more than nationalism and 'liberalism' behind the use of Hungarian.

There were, for instance, social considerations, which seem
to have been entirely overlooked by those who had to deal with
this affair in Rome. Serfdom had been abolished in Hungary
only in 1848, and some landowners, all of them Hungarians,
possessed huge estates, of which some ran to a quarter-million
acres and even more. There was no middle class between the
peasants and the aristocracy, who did not reside on their
estates, the only go-betweens being their stewards, who were
often Jews. The only *élite* among the people at large were
their clergy, who were for the most part married.[7] And what
happened was this: the more capable among the sons of priests
bettered themselves by studying at Hungarian secondary
schools, finishing when possible at the University of Budapest,
and then were ordained or entered on a secular career. Polished
by their experience of towns, magyarized[8] by their whole
education, they not unnaturally despised the surroundings
from which they had come: they thought of themselves as
Hungarian and did not want to speak any other language.
(The same phenomenon existed in Poland, where the Ukrainian gentry had been completely swallowed up; and a similar
thing was to happen in Syria, the Lebanon and Egypt, where
teaching congregations multiplied schools and colleges in
which French was carefully taught at the expense of Arabic,
and the local rite of worship ignored, without anyone bother-
ing about what the result would be.)

These magyarized priests liked to preach only in Hungarian,
and, being very attached to their rite, saw its use in the liturgy
as a means towards satisfying both their ancestral traditions and
their linguistic and political preferences. The educated laity took
the same view. Those people who were not yet magyarized,

supported by many of their clergy, did all they could to resist the change, but they were powerless. There was bound to be a conflict. The Hungarian nationalists knew this well enough, but political passion was too inflamed for them to pay any attention to the possible consequences; those who were unbelievers were pleased at the prospect. Hungary First was the watchword, and inside Hungary, no more diversity; one single language, Hungarian, the language of the gentry and the educated. The time would come when this fanaticism reached such a point that on international trains, where public notices are in several languages, the coaches that were Hungarian property had these notices, and even the menus in the restaurant-car, exclusively in Hungarian. I have seen this myself, many a time.

The Rumanians of Transylvania, which was then part of Hungary, put up the best resistance. To a large extent, Transylvania was the birthplace of the Rumanian renaissance. The Rumanians there had their own schools and colleges, and also went to Bucharest or further afield to study. They were resolved not to be absorbed, however strong the Hungarian pressure. There were no magyarizers among the clergy, though they all knew Hungarian and there were some bilingual villages.

*   *   *

At Rome, no one remembered a problem like this before. The interest in the Christian East that we see today, a consequence of the international eucharistic congress of Jerusalem in 1893, was still in its infancy, and it must be admitted that people were very badly informed. The detailed proceedings of the debates at the Council of Trent had not yet been published; and it was quite natural to cling to chapter viii of the twenty-second session which, without expressly condemning the use of the spoken tongue at Mass, pronounced it to be inexpedient. What we now call the liturgical movement was not yet in existence; and no suggestion for the use of any other language but Latin had been heard in the West for three hundred years.[9]

Pope Leo XIII referred the question to the Congregation for Extraordinary Ecclesiastical Affairs. On 2 September 1896 the congregation published its decision through the Holy Office, evidently with the object of enhancing its effectiveness. The decision was negative. It is interesting to notice that, apart from negativing the power of bishops to authorize such translations, the grounds of the condemnation are just those objections that critics of an exclusive use of Latin have to meet today: ancient tongues are better for maintaining the dignity of sacred rites; living languages change every day; to use them encourages the formation of national churches; the claim that their use enables the faithful to understand the holy Mysteries better is not a sufficient reason, and moreover was declared false and rash by Pope Pius VI, when he condemned the teachings of the Synod of Pistoia in 1786. To these considerations were added that, were Hungarian allowed to the magyarized Ruthenians, the same concession would have to be made to Latin-rite Hungarians.

The Holy See communicated its decision to the Hungarian government before it was made public. In the session of 5 September, the president of the council of ministers, Baron Desiderius Bannfi, told parliament that, before thinking of the erection of a special bishopric, the question of liturgical language must be settled, and he believed it could be done. After all, what would be the use of this bishopric without the Hungarian language in its churches? That shows the government's real aim: to help on the complete magyarization of bilingual areas. The decree of the Holy Office was badly received by Hungarians in general, for they interpreted it as an unfriendly act towards their nationality. It was then that the bishop of Munkacs, Julius Firczak, suggested the enforcement of the official regulation of his predecessor, Basil Popovich: celebration in Staroslav, but with the litanies, epistle and gospel, prayers before communion and all the people's chants in Hungarian.

At the same time the government transmitted a note to the Holy See, in which it declared that the best way of preventing

the Podcarpathian Ruthenians from adhering to the Russian
schism was to let them have their liturgy in Hungarian, just
as the Rumanians had it in Rumanian; for everything else,
said the government, was the same as with the non-Catholics —
rite, calendar, editions of liturgical books. (This last point,
about books, was quite untrue.) The note ignored the fact that
the mountain-dwellers in Podcarpathia definitely did not want
services and preaching in Hungarian, which most of them did
not understand. Leo XIII had this note and Bishop Firczak's
proposal examined by a special commission of the Congregation for Extraordinary Affairs; and its decision, given in March
1897, was simply a confirmation of the previous one. This
second condemnation was followed by a third, in June of the
next year; this was in reply to another official memorandum,
which merely repeated the arguments already advanced by the
government and the bishop of Munkacs.

Three days before this decision was given, on 20 June 1898,
the community council of Budapest, largely composed of lay
people, decided to form a 'national commission' in the capital
itself. Its president was Eugene Jeno, a member of the house
of lords and himself of Ruthenian origin; nevertheless, in
accordance with the psychology that has been explained above,
he was very interested in getting rid of all Slavism. The
Hajdudorog committee was dissolved. Thus, from being
purely local, the question became national. The avowed aim
was simply to obtain the use of Hungarian in the Byzantine
liturgy, no longer in the immediate neighbourhood of
Hajdudorog only, but everywhere where the number of
Hungarian-speaking faithful and their spiritual welfare
required it. It was clear that all bilingual parishes were
threatened. This was so well understood, that of the fifty
parishes that had helped to form the Hajdudorog committee,
thirteen now withdrew; five of them were Rumanian. This
did not prevent the national commission from claiming later
that it had the support of 111 parishes and 135,000 individuals.
It would be interesting to know how this support was
obtained.

Meantime the request for Hungarian was sent to Rome again, and examined for a fourth time. The decision (26 January 1899) was still more severe. The request was not only refused; the Congregation also rejected the possibility even of secondary concessions, to avoid giving any fresh encouragement to the nationalist movement. This was stated in so many words, and the bishops were asked to report annually on this movement. None of them did so, except the bishop of Koros (Krizevci) in Croatia, in whose diocese the movement did not exist. The silence of the Ruthenian bishops of Munkacs and Eperies is understandable, for they were more or less won over to magyarization; but it is surprising that the Rumanian hierarchs said nothing.

In the jubilee year 1900 a carefully organized pilgrimage of Hungarians of Byzantine rite went to Rome. It was led by the bishops of Munkacs and Eperies, and of the 461 pilgrims, 67 were clergy and 96 lay representatives of education and learning. The pilgrimage was received in audience by Leo XIII, and before leaving Rome it transmitted a long petition to the pope; this was drawn up in both Latin and Hungarian, and it asked that Hungarian might be allowed in their liturgy. An imposing commemorative album was afterwards published, containing the text of all the speeches that had been made, except the address of the pope himself, which had been in very general terms; it also contained some large maps showing all the places in Transylvania and the rest of Hungary where Hungarian-speaking Byzantine Catholics were to be found.

The petition to the pope, in a rococo Latin such as only Hungarians know how to write, added a new consideration to its authors' argument. The Hungarians of 'Greek rite', they said, are the descendants of old Greek colonies settled in Hungary during the middle ages. The final section professed to be an enumeration of all the concessions of the spoken tongue in divine worship granted by the Holy See in the course of centuries, especially to the Easterners. This section was swarming with errors, sometimes gross errors, quite apart from the fact that none of these concessions had ever taken place. As for the 'old Greek colonies', I have gone into this question carefully and reached this conclusion: that it could only be a matter of a few monasteries of foreign monks, or of temporary religious missions at a time when Hungary was not yet wholly Christian; these missions flourished for a time, but left no trace behind them. There were indeed colonies of Greek merchants in some towns of northern Hungary; but they were established only during the eighteenth century, and had disappeared entirely by the middle of the nineteenth. I have visited some of their churches and cemeteries, and saw no inscription later than 1850. An examination of the family names of 175 priests of the diocese of Hajdudorog at the time of its greatest extension shows that 54 names are undoubtedly Rumanian, 48 Ruthenian, and of the remaining 73 many are nicknames or from trades and occupations.

The pilgrims' petition was duly examined, and at the same time the Holy See consulted the apostolic nuncio at Vienna and also Father Nicholas Nilles, s.j., professor at the University of Innsbruck, one of the few experts on the subject available in those days. The nuncio did not believe there was a danger of schism, and indeed Russian Orthodox were not really active in Podcarpathia before 1908. In the nuncio's opinion, danger would arise only if Rome formally forbade the use of Hungarian; he advised that the Holy See should not insist, but should in practice tolerate what it could not prevent, without making any explicit pronouncement one way or the other. Father Nilles also was in favour of toleration. Accordingly, on 10 April 1902, a combined session of the Congregations of Extraordinary Affairs and for Spreading the Faith decided not to reply further to the appeals of 1898 and 1900, unless fresh entreaty should be made. In that case, the bishops would be informed that the Holy See maintained its prohibition, but at the same time did not wish to insist on its rigorous observance, provided that there was no growth of the nationalist movement. On the following day Pope Leo XIII approved this decision.

The position remained unchanged until 1909. Meanwhile, in Budapest itself, the priest of the Byzantine church, Emilius Melles, a very active translator of liturgical texts, celebrated regularly in Hungarian; and in that year he was denounced for doing so to the primate of Hungary, Cardinal Claudius Vaszary The cardinal informed the Congregation for the Spreading of the Faith, emphasizing that Father Melles was in a difficult position: quite apart from his own opinions, both the government and the national commission were keeping a sharp eye on him. St Pius X was then pope, and he was a pontiff not disposed to make concessions; he was preoccupied with reforms and the Church's internal organization, and fully involved in the fight against Modernism; and Leo XIII's Eastern policy and interest in the subject were left on one side. The Congregation for the Spreading of the Faith passed Vaszary's information on to the Congregation for Extraordinary Affairs, whose members included several cardinals well known for their intransigence, Oreglia di Santo Stefano, Merry del Val, Vivès y Tuto. Their response was that Cardinal Vaszary should be requested to have the previous condemnations respected. This was to ask for the impossible. The Apponyi Law of two years earlier had enacted that throughout Hungary the sole language of teaching, even in primary schools and for religious instruction, should be Hungarian if the municipality asked for it. Cardinal Vaszary could only shut his eyes and refrain from replying to the Congregation.

But he of course communicated the Congregation's response to Father Melles who, equally of course, did not keep it to himself, but told it all to the president of the national commission, Eugene Szabo. Szabo wanted the new 'Hungarian' diocese at all costs, and he wanted its see to be in his native place —which was Hajdudorog. Under his influence, tactics were changed completely: instead of working for the Hungarian language first, and then the diocese, it was to be the other way round. Get the bishopric first and then the language question could be settled.

The minister for ecclesiastical affairs, John Zichy, was

c

opposed to this change of objective, but he had to give in to Szabo's persistence in the upper house of parliament. A new memorandum was sent to the Holy See, repeating all the arguments of 1900; but this time, instead of speaking of the 'Ruthenian rite' and the 'Rumanian rite', it spoke of the 'Greek rite'. The new terminology was no less misleading than the old, but it was a clever move. The number of Hungarian-speaking Byzantines was now given as 240,000. Since Rome did not want new liturgical languages, fearing complications with Latin-rite Hungarians and others, would she grant the new diocese a neutral tongue, ecclesiastical Greek, since it was a matter affecting the 'Greek' church as distinct from the 'Latin' church? (One can see where the use of such inexact expressions could lead.) If an arrangement could not be come to, there was reason to fear, it was said, that the people concerned, seeing their nationality threatened, might turn Calvinist. With regard to the Hungarian-speaking Szeklers, said to be descended from the Huns of old, their district formed an enclave in the Rumanian archdiocese of Fagaras; for them the government would be satisfied with an episcopal vicariate. In conclusion, the memorandum promised the government's financial support for the endowment of the new 'Greek' bishopric.

A map was annexed to this document, differing from those of 1900. It showed the whole of Hungary as it then was, with the boundaries of the Ruthenian and Rumanian dioceses, indication of all Hungarian-speaking places, and the proposed territory of the new bishopric and Szekler vicariate; the whole was decked out with many colours and special signs to show the majority language, language of preaching, and so on. It is noticeable that many names figuring on the 1900 maps are missing from this one, while others are added to it. One gets the impression that those responsible were trying to show how the territory of the new diocese would comprise a very compact grouping, while a number of Hungarian-speakers were being generously sacrificed. The map was obviously faked; the Ruthenians and Rumanians could have produced

very different ones—and perhaps no more reliable. Since the
outbreak of universal nationalism we have become used to
this sort of thing.[10]

★   ★   ★

The suggestion of Greek for the liturgical language was
designed to make a strong impression at Rome, but only on
the assumption either of bad faith there or of a grave lack of
knowledge of the actual circumstances of the problem. The
clergy concerned knew no Greek, or had forgotten the little
they had ever learned; while as for the people, they did not
know a word of it and would have to give up singing in church.
The pronunciation was what is called Erasmian, so-called 'old'
but really artificial, while the Byzantine music, even as
modified, is based on the Reuchlinian or 'modern' system.
This music has a neumatic notation, difficult to learn properly,
while the Slavs in the sixteenth century adopted Guy of
Arezzo's stave; and there had been further modification and
development on both sides. The only thing available was the
Greek edition of the liturgical books, which had just been
completed in Rome. The promoters of the new scheme were
counting on the Italo-Greek monks of Grottaferrata, near
Rome, to initiate the Basilian monks at the sanctuary of Maria-
Pocs into the new language; but at this time Grottaferrata had
only a dozen members, nearly all old, ignorant of Hungarian,
and little disposed to expatriate themselves. The Hungarian
Basilians were not in much better case. In short, the imposition
of Greek was likely to cause far-reaching trouble. Moreover,
while only seven Rumanian parishes, totalling about seven
thousand souls, had adhered to the petition of the year 1900,
claim was now to be laid to eighty-three Rumanian parishes.
Before coming to a decision, Rome consulted the whole
Hungarian episcopate, at the time of its plenary conference at
Budapest in November 1911. The Ruthenian bishops, of
Munkacs, Eperies and Koros, were resigned to the government's wishes. Of the four Rumanian sees, one was vacant
through death. It was foreseen that the nineteen residential

and titular bishops of Hungary proper would not oppose a measure which did not concern or interest them. The question of the new diocese was brought up in the middle of other matters. The primate, Cardinal Vaszary, declared that it was simply a matter of principle—one more Byzantine-rite diocese would be advantageous to Hungary; since the 'Latin' church uses Latin in its liturgy, it seemed only natural that the 'Greek' church should return to its mother tongue. The three Rumanian bishops were faced by some thirty others, all favourable or indifferent to the scheme, and good care was taken not to tell the Rumanians how many parishes they stood to lose. However, these three drew up two memoranda: one was for the papal nuncio, who was new to his office and not yet well informed about these complex matters; the other was for the president of the council of ministers, requesting that they, the Rumanian bishops, should at least be consulted on the subject of parishes of which it was proposed they should be deprived.

The government vouchsafed no reply to this, and resolved to negotiate, not with the Congregation for the Spreading of the Faith, which might 'know too much', but with Pope Pius X personally. The Rumanians allege that the Hungarian government dangled before the Pope's eyes a promise of the King-Emperor Francis Joseph that he would take under his exalted patronage the international eucharistic congress to be held at Vienna in 1912. The government certainly multiplied its undertakings: only non-liturgical services would be held in the Hungarian language; the clergy should have three years to learn Greek; in those parishes where Hungarian was not in use liturgically, Staroslav or Rumanian would go on being used for three years, but no longer. Upholders of Greek counted a lot on the papal secretary of state, Cardinal Merry del Val, who was very opposed to the use of Hungarian in public worship. In February 1912 the secretariate of state consulted Cardinal Gotti, prefect of the Congregation for the Spreading of the Faith; he could not refrain from expressing his scepticism about the success of all this changing of languages. But before he had time to dispatch his reply, the official gazette *Budapesti Hirlap* was waving the flag of victory and informing its readers that opposition to the Hungarian language came from—the Council of Florence of 1439!

When invited by the secretariate of state at Rome to make concrete observations about the parishes to be aggregated to the new diocese, the three Rumanian bishops did not know what to say; and they confined themselves to declaring that the project would compromise the chances of a future re-union of the Orthodox Church of Rumania with the Holy See (a very problematical happening anyway). The govern-ment was in a hurry for the business to be settled, and the papal nuncio invited these bishops to a conference at Budapest. The metropolitan was old and ill; his delegate (and future succes-sor), Canon Basil Suciu, missed his train, and did not warn the other two bishops. They, not knowing quite what was expected of them, brought up a decree of their provincial council of 1872, which forbade the taking of serious decisions without the advice and approval of the metropolitan; they therefore proposed a further conference to which repre-sentatives of each of the dioceses concerned should be invited.

In January 1912, Canon Suciu went to Rome on behalf of his metropolitan; there he was assured that only a Ruthenian bishopric was in question, that Budapest's written promises about the use of Hungarian could be relied on, and that the liturgical language would be Greek. In the following March, the two other Rumanian bishops went to Rome, one after the other, and he of Gherla, Basil Hossu, revealed to St Pius X all the Hungarian government's double-dealing. 'They have deceived me!' exclaimed the Pope, and ordered an immediate revision of the bull of erection, which was already drawn up. But Budapest went on raising difficulties through its ambassador at the Vatican, who represented the Rumanian bishops' objections to be frivolous and without support from the lower clergy and people.[11] The Emperor Francis Joseph had promised his fullest support for the eucharistic congress at Vienna, and Cardinal Merry del Val was convinced that with the Greek language everything would work out for the best.

Accordingly, the bull establishing the diocese of Hajdudorog, *'Christifideles graeci ritus'*, appeared on 8 June 1912. It recalled the establishment of the Rumanian ecclesiastical province in 1853, observed that the new diocese would help Catholics to spread their faith among their dissident Rumanian neighbours, and again condemned the use of Hungarian in the liturgy; for the rest, it met all the wishes of the Hungarian government. The parishes allotted to the new see numbered 162, of which 78 were Ruthenian and 83 Rumanian; the other one was the mixed parish at Budapest, which until then had belonged to the primatial see of Esztergom. Many of these parishes were in fact bilingual, which increased the triumph of the Hungarian government. It had obtained half of what it wanted, and the introduction of Greek would never get beyond the stage of promises.

* * *

What followed was bound to follow, and could have been in part avoided only if from the start authoritative consideration had been given to the Eastern principle concerning liturgical language; and if Rome had been better informed about the factors in Hungary, to enable the politicians' traps to be avoided. In the parliament at Bucharest and in the Orthodox Rumanian press, both of the Old Kingdom and of Transylvania, Pope Pius X was held up as the great enemy of Rumanian nationality. There was hardly any Catholic periodical in Rumanian, except the *Univrea* of Blaj, a little daily sheet read by hardly anybody outside the clergy. This paper could not take sides against Rome, nor could it simply say nothing, but it had no policy of its own. All it could do was to support the suggestion of the well-known Orthodox historian Nicholas Iorga,[12] namely, to have recourse to the principle of double jurisdiction and found Rumanian parishes wherever any part of the population still spoke Rumanian. But the Hungarian government had foreseen this scheme when it put under the jurisdiction of Hajdudorog a territory without other solution of continuity than that of the Szekler vicariate; Iorga's idea could not be implemented without support from Rome, on which it was idle to count after the publication of the bull.

There had been public demonstrations even before the publication, notably at Alba Julia on 29 May 1912, in which more than twenty-five thousand people took part; but it all ended in talk, as the Hungarians knew it would. The temporary administrator of Hajdudorog was the bishop of Munkacs, Antony Papp, whose Hungarian sympathies were very marked. He sent around to a number of villages a priest inspector of schools, of Ruthenian origin but no less ardent a magyarizer, who took policemen with him and questioned the Rumanian parish-priests. Arrests followed, and prosecutions which ended in priests being deprived of their appointments for three years and more. In one village the people would not go to church, and buried their dead without religious rites rather than avail themselves of a priest from Hajdudorog.

The first bishop of the new see was Stephen Miklosy; he was nominated by the sovereign, in accordance with the concordat of 1855, and confirmed by the Holy See in 1913. There was no question of his residing at Hajdudorog; this town had a population of ten thousand (almost all Byzantine Catholics), but when the present writer visited it in 1923 the streets were not even paved. So the bishop settled at Debreczen, and here in February 1914 an attempt was made on his life by two Russian nihilists, at whose instigation is not certainly known. The exploding bomb did not hurt the bishop, but it killed the school-inspector mentioned above. The episcopal residence was then moved to the neighbouring town of Nyiregyhaza, where it still is; there I talked with Bishop Miklosy and his clergy in 1923.

Rumanian deputies in the Hungarian parliament protested against the violence and legal proceedings to which reference has been made, but it was in vain. An attempt was made in 1913 to realize Nicholas Iorga's proposal by means of an act of parliament; but it was opposed by the new Hungarian primate, Cardinal Csernoch (himself of Slovak origin), and it came to nothing. After the attempt on Bishop Miklosy's life there was much talk of Hajdudorog in the European press, but within a few months there came the assassination of the Archduke Francis Ferdinand at Sarajevo that started the first World War, and silence fell.

It will be readily understood that nothing came of the liturgy in Greek. As there was only a limited supply of the requisite books in the Roman edition, it was understood that the Hungarian government would pay for a reprint. Nothing was done about this, but special editions of the *Hieratikon*[13] were published in 1912 and 1920. In this book the anaphora of the Liturgy (equivalent to the canon of the Mass) was printed in both languages, Greek and Hungarian, on opposite pages. But I have been able to ascertain for myself that only the Hungarian is used, except for the words of consecration: these are chanted in Greek, with the Erasmian pronunciation; the impression produced is rather curious. In 1915 Bishop Miklosy asked for an extension of four and a half years before Greek should become obligatory; Pope Benedict XV agreed, but eight years later the clergy knew no more than before, as my own experience showed. Since then, the same state of things has continued, opposition to the use of Hungarian has ceased, and today there is probably not a single Greek liturgical book in Hungary outside the bigger libraries.

*   *   *

After the collapse of Hungary in the first World War, the Rumanians lost no time in recovering the parishes that had been taken from them. In November 1918 the Rumanian consistory at Blaj[14] instituted a vicariate at Targul-Mures (Marosvasarhely) for the Szekler country, the clergy from Hajdudorog having fled when Rumanian troops occupied Transylvania; this *fait accompli* was sanctioned by the nuncio at Vienna in 1919. As the Szeklers speak only Hungarian, the Orthodox archbishop of Bucharest later on formed a project of sending priests there to try to rumanianize them. Hearing this, the Catholic metropolitan of Fagaras, Basil Suciu at once dispatched all the clergy he could spare to look after these Catholics. But they did not know enough Hungarian, and after a few weeks came back in despair to Blaj, saying they had been unable either to hear confessions or to preach and talk to the people. Hajdudorog was still in Hungary, but over half its parishes were now in Rumania. Article 3 of the concordat between the Holy See and Rumania (1927) stipulated that[1] no part of the Rumanian kingdom should depend on a bishop whose see was outside the Rumanian frontiers'. Accordingly, by a decree of the Sacred Eastern Congregation[15] in 1934, the dioceses of Fagaras, Oradea Mare and Maramures definitively received back all the parishes of which they had been deprived in 1912. Gherla had already been given its four parishes back in 1922. The liturgical use of Rumanian had of course been restored in all these parishes.

Thus the diocese of Hajdudorog was reduced to the boundaries of the former vicariate, which it ought never to have exceeded. The question of liturgical language was again raised, and this time those concerned were carefully consulted: the nuncio at Budapest, the Hungarian primate, the bishop of Hajdudorog. The Hungarians had been chastened by military defeat and raised no difficulties. But in any case there seemed to be general agreement that to introduce Greek entirely was impossible, and that neither the clergy nor the laity concerned any longer knew Slavonic; to attempt to reintroduce the latter in spite of that would only upset the much-tried Hungarians and might lead to serious defections: so the best course seemed to be to leave things as they were, insisting only that the anaphora be said in Greek. Nevertheless, in August 1922, the Eastern Congregation in Rome decided to require the total adoption of Greek. But it was not practicable to do so, and this was eventually recognized and the subject was allowed to drop. Hungarian is still forbidden in theory, but it is tolerated in fact; even the Basilians of Maria-Pocs and elsewhere have had to yield. Seven years later, as we shall see, Pope Pius XI took a different line with regard to Estonian and sanctioned the Eastern principle; it is a sound principle, but politics must not be allowed to intrude upon it.

Hitler's *diktat* of Vienna on 1 September 1940, by which all Podcarpathia and half Transylvania were returned to Hungary, threw everything into confusion again. The Hungarians began to be restive, and were said to want to make Hajdudorog a metropolitan see; and a Hungarian bishopric of dissident Orthodox was set up, though it had very few members. Had such a project gone through it would probably have led to a mass apostasy of the Ruthenians in Podcarpathia, who wanted above all to keep their own nationality and Slav character. Russian Orthodox activity had been intensifying there since 1908, and there had been sixty thousand defections in the diocese of Mukachevo (Munkacs) between 1920 and 1923.[16] The diocese of Preshov (Eperies), of which a good part is Slovak, was more resistant, through the energy of the bishop of Krizevci (Koros), Dionysius Nyaradi, who was at that time adminstering Preshov. Since the second World War, Podcarpathia has been under the yoke of the U.S.S.R., and it is impossible to foretell the future. In 1947 the bishop of Mukachevo, the holy Theodore Romza, died after a traffic collision that was manifestly deliberate; in 1949 many priests were deported to Russia and Siberia; in 1950 the bishop of Preshov, Paul Gojdich, and his auxiliary, Basil Hopko, were thrown into jail: they are still there, and the dioceses have been aggregated to the patriarchate of Moscow. The people passively resist as best they can, but they have no bishops and the time will come when they have no priests, even in hiding.

There is still a bishop at Hajdudorog, but for how much longer?[17] Communist governments intend to wipe out every vestige of Catholicity of Eastern rite in their territories, while taking every opportunity to suppress Western Catholics, too. Little news penetrates from beyond the 'iron curtain', but God is there and his enemies can do nothing against him.

*   *   *

We may now ask ourselves what could properly have been done had it not been for the influence of a disposition of the Council of Trent which did not refer to the East and was at variance with Eastern tradition; and even more, had it not been for the untoward irruption of secular politics.

The use of Hungarian is wholly in accordance with that Eastern principle concerning liturgical language which has been several times referred to; Hungarian is as legitimate as Arabic and Rumanian, to instance only the two living tongues adopted without dispute in relatively recent times. If there is a clergy and a laity who do not know and understand either Staroslav or Rumanian, and who moreover have a marked antipathy for both those tongues, they cannot be forced to use them. To want to replace them by Greek is utopian, and to try to do so would be to destroy the admirable custom of the people taking an active and truly communal part in public worship. The popular demand for Hungarian was one of those spontaneous movements which in themselves are in no way contrary to faith or morals, and those movements are very powerful; it is much better to control and regulate them than to try to smother them.

The establishment of the diocese of Hajdudorog served no useful purpose. It would have been sufficient to keep the episcopal vicariate that existed after 1873, if necessary forming one or two others, thus applying the principle of unity of episcopal hierarchy with plurality of parishes according to their national composition. Parishes that were wholly Hungarian-speaking would have presented no difficulty. In places of mixed population, necessarily more or less bilingual, where a substantial part of the people needed the liturgy in Hungarian, there would have had to be organized parishes with both territorial and personal jurisdiction. That was the solution advocated by the Rumanian Nicholas Iorga. The experience

of the Rumanian priests sent from Blaj to the Szeklers shows
that this was the only way out of the difficulty.

It was also necessary that a Hungarian version of all the
Byzantine liturgical books should have been put in hand,
beginning with the *Hieratikon*, a complete *Horologion*, a
Eukhologion or Ritual, and a proper Epistle and Gospel book,
so that the clergy should not have to read the liturgical lessons
from any copy of the New Testament that happened to be
handy. All this could have been done without neglecting the
provision of prayer-books for the people.

It is a very great pity that it was not done. Mention has
been made of the Hungarian version of the Liturgy of St John
Chrysostom brought out by George Kricsfalusi at Ungvar
as early as 1795, and clearly intended for liturgical use. But it
was after 1850 that the demand for Hungarian books increased
more and more. The Chrysostom Liturgy, with additions,
was reprinted at Debreczen in 1882; and in the same year there
was reissued an incomplete Ritual, in a translation published
at Hajdudorog in 1879; this was reprinted at Ungvar in 1907.
The Liturgy of St Basil, with supplements for Lent, appeared
at Hajdudorog in 1890. Father Melles, to whom reference has
been made, in 1905 published the first volume of an abridged
edition of the *Menaia*, or Sanctoral, which he translated from
the Greek of the Roman edition, under the title of *Anthologion*;
but it contained only September and October, and the rest has
never appeared. Mention has already been made above of the
complete *Hieratikon* first published at Nyiregyhaza in 1912,
with the anaphora in both Greek and Hungarian. A book
containing all the parts of various offices habitually sung by
the people was published by Ignatius Roskovich at Debreczen
in 1862; it has been reissued several times.

In 1938 there appeared at Miskolc a work labelled *Zsoloszma*,
Psalter, whose proper title is the 'Book of Prayers and Chants'.
It consists of twelve separate parts, with a binding-case into
which each monthly part can be inserted as required. This is
largely a translation of the Greek *Horologion*, or Ordinary of
the Divine Office, but without all the usual supplements. The

ferial office for each day of the week is shortened, as is the 'common of saints'; on the other hand, the book contains a number of things that are useful only to the laity, and 'hybridisms' are not lacking. Nor is the book well arranged, so that it is rather difficult to use. The preface says that its object is to combine a book of public worship for Sundays and feasts with a sort of breviary for the clergy, though they are not bound to private Office. The preface adds that Cardinal Sincero accepted the dedication of the first part of the book, encouraged its continuance, and offered the translators a copy of each of the Greek books published in Rome. As Cardinal Sincero was secretary of the Eastern Congregation at that time, this makes it clear that in practice the Holy See is no longer opposing the liturgical use of Hungarian.

We see then that the Byzantine Hungarians, while having what is needed for ordinary parochial occasions, are very far from having a sufficiently complete translation of their liturgical texts, even in a reasonable abridged form.[18] And the clergy will have to make do with this truncated liturgy all the while they remain under communist domination, if their church is able to survive so long. It was a disaster that political and nationalist passion was ever imported into the language question, and the same mistake must be sedulously avoided when better times return. Nobody knows what the future holds; but if in time to come Hungary includes an element of ethnic foreigners, all will be well in the diocese of Hajdudorog if all are treated with tolerance and a full understanding.

CHAPTER THREE

LATER DEVELOPMENTS IN THE EAST

DURING the past hundred years or so the principle of using the local tongue in public worship has been frequently applied in the Orthodox Church, and on a small scale here and there by Eastern Catholics; in the previous chapter we have seen the circumstances of the most important example among these last.

The Russians led the way. Alone among the Orthodox, they had, and still have, though on a very reduced scale since the revolution of 1917, foreign missions like those of the Catholic Church: missions in the first place to remote non-Christian peoples within their own vast empire, and then to the Chinese, the Japanese, the Koreans.[1] The results of these missions can hardly be compared with those of the Catholic Church: on the one hand because of a certain inadequacy in some of the missionaries and their methods; on the other, because of a chronic interference by the imperial government and a consequent bureaucratic system. However, we are concerned with them here only from the point of view of liturgical languages.

It was not till the proclamation of a partial freedom of conscience in 1905 that a serious movement of interior reform could be made manifest in the Russian Church, and it led eventually to the restoration of the patriarchate of Moscow in 1918. Once the imperial censorship was relaxed it began to be publicly acknowledged that all was far from being well with the Church of Russia, and demands for reforms, often radical, were heard from many different voices. This movement has by no means been wholly stifled by the violent persecution carried on for years by the communists, or by the state of slavery under which the Russian Church has existed since the government found it more expedient to use her as a tool.

It is not surprising that one of the measures advocated was the substitution of the Russian language for Staroslav in the liturgy. People took sides about this, and it is interesting to notice that both sides used the same arguments that are heard today in the West with reference to Latin. Attempts to effect this change have been made by the bodies that have one after another detached themselves from the patriarchal church, but they have had no more success than have those bodies themselves. Staroslav continues to be the liturgical language of the Russian patriarchate. The only modification is that ordinary Russian characters are used instead of the Cyrillic alphabet; but this is a matter of necessity, and confined to small books, for liturgical books properly so called are no longer printed in Russia.

The first Russian to use a local tongue in the liturgy seems to have been St Stephen, bishop of Perm, who died in 1396;[2] his aim was to facilitate the conversion of the heathen Zyrian, who lived below the Urals to the south-west. An archbishop of Kazan, Ambrose Protasov (d. 1826), revived this idea, but was not able to put it into effect. In 1846, Tsar Nicholas I authorized translations into the language of the Tartars and of other peoples. A Tartar version of the Chrysostom Liturgy was made in 1866, and used for the first time at Kazan two years later. In 1883 the governing synod of the Russian Church ordered that such work of translation should be pushed on; by 1892, the eucharistic Liturgy was being celebrated in Chuvash and in Tartar in over a hundred churches, sometimes with a mixture of Staroslav.

The great difficulty about these translations, which only include certain essential texts, is this: such a tongue as Tartar is fairly well developed, but it has two forms, as is found elsewhere in the East. One is polished and correct, strewn with Persian and Arabic words, but understood only by the more educated, and in any case not very good for expressing Christian ideas; the other is a common speech, spoken by the people at large and limited to the needs of daily life. The translator has therefore to find a middle way between these, to be at the same time both correct and understandable. The same difficulty attends fully evolved languages, Arabic, for instance.[3] As for the tongues of the other mid-Asiatic and Siberian peoples, they are still impoverished languages, without grammatical discipline, and it is very difficult to make anything presentable of them.

Originally these translations had nothing but a wholly religious object: to attract non-Christians to Christianity. There were others besides those mentioned. A version of the eucharistic Liturgy appeared in Chinese in 1866, and was republished in 1894. The mission to Japan, begun in 1861 and today numbering some fifty thousand faithful, with an almost entirely Japanese clergy, has several liturgical books in Japanese. The first celebration in that language was in 1873, and by 1895 a second edition of the three Liturgies was called for.

But imperial politics was not slow in rearing its head: there were translations into Estonian and Latvian (Lettish) in 1844 and, at a date I cannot ascertain exactly, into Finnish and the Eskimo dialect. In Bessarabia, the printing of liturgical books in Rumanian was first authorized and then forbidden; in Georgia, the government made every effort to impose Staroslav on the town churches, relegating Georgian to the villages. Until the fall of the tsardom in 1917, the general policy was this: the liturgical use of their own tongues was allowed to 'backward' peoples, because this helped to bring them to the Orthodox faith; they could be russified later; but Staroslav was forced on non-Russians who had a developed culture of their own in order to hasten their russification. An analogous state of affairs was to be found in Poland when a self-governing Orthodox church was organized there after the first World War. In order to keep the goodwill of a very nationalistic government, the metropolitan and his synod allowed celebrations in Polish; while to satisfy the Byelorussians, who were calling for ethnic autonomy, they were allowed to use their own language.

Elsewhere, translations were made for the benefit of Russians who had lost their own speech, as in several parishes around Berlin. Between the wars, the patriarchate of Moscow established a French Orthodox mission in Paris, with the help of a formerly Catholic priest of some learning and considerable ability. I was present at a celebration of the Liturgy in their little church in 1950. It is all in French, and professes to be a restoration of the 'Western rite'; in fact, it is an adaptation of the Roman Mass with Byzantine additions; the chant is substantially that of the Russians.[4]

The Orthodox Ukrainians over wide areas have sought to celebrate the liturgy in their own tongue, which is a sister language to Russian and Byelorussian. Only a few offices besides the eucharistic Liturgy have been translated, and these versions are not always in harmony as regards either morphology, spelling or meaning. They are a result of a movement that seems to be much more nationalist than religious.

The Byzantine Mass was printed in Albanian about 1860 at Bucharest, but their great translator is Bishop Fan (Theophanes) Noli; between 1908 and 1931 he published, first at Boston in the United States and then at Koritza and Tirana in Albania, a series of nine liturgical books; I may be excused from giving their titles in Albanian, which, though a brother to Greek and Latin, is yet profoundly different from both. Those who know this tongue say that the language of these versions is good and the translation exact, and that Kyr Fan Noli has been careful to observe the rhythm of the Constantinopolitan music.[5] The New Testament was translated long since, and without having displaced Greek altogether, Albanian is being increasingly used in church. The Catholic Italo-Albanians have remained outside this movement; why, will be explained later. Of their four colonies in Sicily, one has lost its language completely; but the others still put up a good fight against the growing invasion of Italian, and make modest attempts to use Albanian in church. At the eucharistic Liturgy the people make certain responses in Albanian, and use it for singing the rosary and in some other devotions; but

D

everything else is in Greek, and they do not understand a word of it.

Here and there on certain occasions Catholic Easterners make use of the speech of the country for the scriptural lessons, Creed, Lord's Prayer and prayers before communion, especially when the congregation present is mostly of Latin rite. In a few churches this is the regular practice and, as might be expected, it gets as much welcome as disapproval. I have even heard of the Liturgy being celebrated entirely in French. In North and South America some Melkite priests would like to have the diaconal litanies in English or Spanish, and it is likely that some are now doing so. When appealed to, ecclesiastical authority allows these practices; in itself and in virtue of the Eastern principle there is nothing to object to in this toleration, provided the translation used is correct and approved as such. There can be no doubt that if Eastern rites are to survive in, for example, the United States, it will one day be necessary to authorize them in English. Where Ukrainians or Ruthenians are not living in a compact body they are ceasing to understand Slavonic, and younger generations are growing up to speak only English. They do not go to Western churches because they cannot follow the Latin rite, and sometimes for other reasons; so there is danger of their resorting to a dissident church where the language difficulty is met, or of passing over to Protestantism, or of falling away from religion altogether.[6]

There is one language that so far nobody seems to have thought of making use of; one which nevertheless would seem very convenient for those 'Eastern days' that the Holy See recommends and indeed prescribes for seminaries, with the object of dispelling prejudice and giving at least some very elementary knowledge of Eastern Christian things. The essentials of such days are a conference and a liturgical celebration, according to the personnel available. In practice, the Liturgy is usually in Greek or Staroslav, and the young clerics who assist do so as best they can with the help of a printed or other translation. A proper choir is rarely available, and one has to be arranged *ad hoc*, with the help of texts transliterated into roman characters and music in European notation. But there are excellent *Latin* translations of the Liturgy of St. John Chrysostom, beginning with the one published by the Greeks at Venice in the seventeenth–eighteenth century, and others since. Why not celebrate in Latin, just as is done so well in Rumanian, a language of Latin derivation? The chant could be easily adapted and transcribed, into Gregorian notation or on a five-line stave, which would be as familiar to the students as the Latin. A deacon could be practised to fulfil that office, which adds much to the impressiveness of a Byzantine cele-bration; and a temporary free-standing altar set up with two large pictures of our Lord and his Mother to represent the absent eikonostasis. The seminarists would then be able to understand what was going on and follow it much better. I put forward the suggestion for consideration.

Pope Pius XI's Sanction of the Eastern Principle

In 1929 there was a young Orthodox Estonian priest who was anxious to be reconciled with the Catholic Church in order to work for the return of those of his countrymen who had fallen into Protestant errors and for the union of those who were still Orthodox. He was strongly of the opinion that many of them would become Catholics if the liturgy were celebrated in Estonian, as the Orthodox Estonians had been doing for over seventy-five years. Politics did not enter into it at all, though the Estonians had an antipathy for the Russians and did not like their very long offices, which they tailored to suit themselves. In two successive audiences, Pope Pius XI declared that, were this priest to be reconciled, he would be at liberty to celebrate in Staroslav pending a further decision, and that this question of Estonian was to be gone into.

It must be recognized that the situation was totally different from that at the time of the Hungarian problem in 1896. Quite apart from his remarkable general learning, Pius XI had been nuncio at Warsaw, where he had been initiated into the problems of Russia and had even learned some Russian.

Ideas had undergone considerable development, and though
no one was yet talking about liturgy in living languages for
the West, the customs of the East were now better known.
The question was one for the pontifical Commission for
Russia, which had been set up within the Sacred Eastern
Congregation in 1925.

I shall not be giving away any great secret when I say that it
was the present writer who was entrusted with the duty of
studying the matter. I probed it to the bottom, for the West
as well as the East, making use of all the information I could
then find; my report was the first draft of this present book.
(It is curious that, in the haste of drawing it up, I neglected to
include Theodore Balsamon's formulation of the Eastern
principle concerning liturgical language.)

The *relator* for the commission hardly did more than
summarize my exposition, but he added a number of points.
The first was, that no law, divine, natural or positive, put any
limit to the number of languages which could be used in
public worship. He noted that, earlier on, the nuncio at
Budapest had told him that he did not know any way in which
the Holy See's directions about Hungarian could be enforced;
that the liturgy celebrated in Hungarian was more firmly
established than ever, and that Greek was out of the question.
The *relator* pointed out that the Russian governing synod had
allowed the use of Estonian, even though it would result in a
lessening of Russian prestige, because otherwise the Estonian
Orthodox would have turned Protestant in order to be able to
worship in a language they understood. The principle should
be applied that was admitted for all peoples of an Eastern rite
who become Catholic: their liturgical translations are accepted,
subject only to the correction of errors if there be any. It was
not possible to impose Slavonic, Russian or Greek. Latin
might be suggested, but in that case, said the *relator*, the
Estonians would have to change their rite, which was contrary
to the declarations of the Holy See; and their clergy would
have to learn Latin, of which they were ignorant, and that
was a very difficult matter. So there was nothing against

allowing Estonian; rather did it present the possibility of an abundant harvest.

Of the seven members of the Commission for Russia, four seemed favourable *a priori*; they were Cardinal Sincero, its president; Mgr Michel d'Herbigny, its *relator*; Mgr Carlo Margotti, its secretary; and Kyr Isaias Papadopoulos, honorary assessor of the Eastern Congregation. I do not know the opinions of the others. The plenary session took place on 14 February 1929. The rescript was very encouraging:

' *Dilata, et ad mentem.* The *mens* is, that priests of the Byzantine rite may hope for the use of the Estonian language in the celebration of the holy Liturgy. Meanwhile, the liturgical books must be carefully examined to make sure that there is a worthy translation free from all error. Moreover, it may be granted that in those parts of the holy Liturgy not said in a low voice, the people also sing and respond to the celebrant in their own tongue.'

In the immediate case of the priest who wished to become a Catholic, he could celebrate with the existing version, after correction of any errors. It is obvious that dogmatic errors were here referred to.

This rescript was submitted to the Pope on the following 20 February. I was well acquainted with Pius XI's habits. Several days in advance he always required to have the printed statement of the case, so that he could study it if he wanted to. Otherwise, he was content with the *foglio d'ufficio*, in which the matter in hand is summarized in more or less detail. Especially in the earlier years of his pontificate, Pius XI often delayed his decisions to enable him to read the whole of the relevant statements, which were sometimes voluminous; and he continued to do this whenever a particular matter was of special interest to him. He was always very concerned with anything to do with the Eastern church, and it is most likely that he read the whole of the statement about the Estonian language, although it ran to sixty-four pages of print. But what particularly makes me think he read it is that a clause in the rescript that

he dictated in audience seems to have been taken word for
word from the concluding part of the *relator's* report. Here is
a translation of this rescript of Pius XI, which is of capital
importance for cases of this kind:

> *Adprobantur i et ii, ad mentem.* The *mens* is, that the first point
> must *not* [emphasized in the original] be understood as a re-
> striction of principle in the faculty that the Easterners have of
> using in the liturgy those languages that are best adapted to
> the greater good of souls, if the Holy See approves their use.
> The second point is understood as a grant of the Estonian
> language *per viam facti,* [a grant] which will be able to be used
> as a precedent in similar cases.[7]

In consequence of all this, I was asked to examine a book
sent by the internuncio in Latvia in support of his request: it
was the Estonian translation of the Slavonic *Sluzebnik,* containing the ordinary of Vespers, Matins and the three Liturgies.
I did not know Estonian, a very difficult language belonging
to the Finnish family, but a careful comparison soon showed
me that this version of the corresponding Staroslav was
complete. The latter was free from dogmatic error, and the
Estonian version had been approved by the Russian holy synod,
which was most scrupulous in these matters. The only
corrections required then were the deletion of the names of
members of the Russian imperial family and the putting of the
memorial of the ecclesiastical authority before that of the civil
authority. The first of these had been done in practice by the
Estonians themselves since 1917, and the second was not
absolutely necessary. The book could be trusted, provided
that an examination of the phraseology showed it to be
appropriate; at that time no one could be found in Rome
qualified to pronounce on this.

I do not know if the priest who had occasioned these things
persevered in his intention; but in any case the Soviet armies
eventually invaded Estonia and Catholic work there was
ruined.[8] Some years after 1930 there was a former student of
the Russian College (*Russicum*) at Rome, who had been

intended for Estonia, had visited the country, and had learned something of its language; he undertook to revise the Estonian version of the Chrysostom Liturgy, with the help of two young Estonians who it was at one time hoped would become priests. Twenty-five mimeographed copies were made of this revision, and they were used at two celebrations in the church of the *Russicum* during 1939. The printed original is to be found in the archives of the Commission for Russia, and I presented one of the copies to the library of the Pontifical Oriental Institute.

*   *   *

Pope Pius XI's rescript in this matter suggests reflexions about the use of a living tongue in certain circumstances. We know that Balsamon simply requires that the translation should be accurate, without referring to approval. Whenever a church of Eastern rite is in question, the Holy See has never given this approval formally, but has simply accepted what was in existence. The only exception is the case of Hungarian; we have seen why, and how the prohibition has remained in-effective. I have also mentioned the fact that, especially in countries where the majority is of Latin rite, there are priests who would like to read the scriptural lessons and sing the litanies and other prayers in the spoken tongue; some have done so, and still do so. Pius XI decided that the approval of any new language is reserved to the Holy See: does this apply to these particular cases?

In my opinion, this reservation applies only to the adoption of a language for liturgical worship as a whole. I do not think it applies to passages of limited extent which do not affect the form of sacraments, provided, of course, that the version has received ordinary ecclesiastical approval. I am thinking of such things as the scriptural lessons (which in the East are not read privately by the celebrant while the lector and deacon chant them), the diaconal litanies, the Creed, the Lord's Prayer, the prayers before communion (which, at any rate in Russian usage, are said aloud by the celebrant over the people, after saying them privately before his own communion). In doubtful cases, one would certainly do well to consult the local bishop, and I do not believe it exceeds his powers to grant the approbation asked. The Eastern church has always been much more liberal in this matter than the Western church. Such is my personal opinion. It may surprise those who are used to an exclusive liturgical language, such as Latin; but I think that in a matter of this kind it is appropriate to look at the spirit of a grant or refusal more closely than at its letter.

When it is a question of a language that is quite new to liturgical use, and of using it in public worship as a whole, then it is clear that the approval of the Holy See is necessary. Strictly speaking, that approval was not absolutely required for Estonian: the example of Rumanian shows that Rome has always accepted the relevant practice of a church that is returning to Catholic unity, without concerning herself with its origins.

Could Ukrainian be one day similarly approved, seeing that its recent adoption by the Orthodox in some places is due, not so much to dissatisfaction with Staroslav as such, as to political and social considerations? There is nothing against it in itself, if agreement could be reached on the versions, which at present differ a lot from one another, though all apparently reproducing the original correctly. The only objections would be that political antipathy for the Russians is not an adequate reason, and that Staroslav is very close to Ukrainian. However, there are certain historical circumstances that could be appealed to. During the first Russian occupation in 1939–1941, there was a movement among the Orthodox towards reunion with Rome in many places, from Kiev to Byelorussia. The Catholic Ukrainian metropolitan, Andrew Szepticky, set himself to encourage this and formed a plan of action; it came to nothing, and in any case would have been killed when the Russian armies finally returned to Galicia in 1944.[9] But it had been provided that, in parishes that should declare themselves Catholic and where the liturgy was conducted in Ukrainian, Byelorussian or any other language, these languages would be respected and kept. The people were now used to them, and it is very difficult to alter the habits of peasants.

Malayalam in Malabar

The last language used in any notable degree in Eastern liturgy is *Malayalam*, in the Malabar region of the south-west coast of India.

The languages of the Indian peninsula are divided into two principal large groups: those called Dravidian, belonging to the primitive inhabitants, and those of the Aryans, who came from the north-east and perhaps drove the Dravidians into the southern part. The chief Dravidian tongues are Tamil, Telugu, Kanarese and Malayalam. Their origin is uncertain; it has been sought to establish a relationship with the Sumerian of ancient Chaldea.[10] The fundamental Aryan language was Sanskrit, now dead, but the mother of the Indo-European family of tongues. From it is derived Western Hindi or Hindustani, the most widely diffused Indian speech, which has been made the official language of the republic of India. The idiom called Urdu is used by many in Pakistan; it is a literary form of colloquial Hindustani that arose from the Mohammedan domination; it has a large vocabulary of Arabic and Persian words, and is written in Arabic-Persian characters. The other languages mentioned have each their own characters, the Malayalam alphabet running to fifty-six letters or combinations. It is a rich language, well developed grammatically, and capable of expressing fine shades of thought; it has a good and ancient literary tradition. A considerable proportion of its vocabulary has been borrowed from Sanskrit.

I have already had occasion to refer to the Christians of Malabar when speaking of Syriac in Chapter One above, and I shall have to come back to them again in Part III. The largest body among them, generally called simply the Catholic Malabarese, have been under a strictly Western discipline for over three hundred years, and so have maintained Syriac as their sole liturgical language. The interrogations at baptism and at marriage take place twice, first in Syriac, then in Malayalam. At the eucharistic Liturgy all is in Syriac, the celebrant reading the scriptural lessons in a low voice while a reader reads them aloud in the vernacular. At a 'children's Mass', a lay person reads out translations of some of the prayers. For the rest, silence reigns among the faithful, unless the rosary be said aloud. There are Malayalam prayer-books available, partly versions of liturgical texts, partly 'methods of hearing Mass', just as they are known in the West. The Chaldean or East Syrian Divine Office, much altered, is said in Syriac by the clergy, beginning at the subdiaconate. Further particulars will be given in Part III. Good Syriac scholars are rare, for the language gets little attention in the seminaries, which are directed by religious of the Latin rite; many of the clergy know little about it, and the laity nothing at all. But there are now the small beginnings of a movement to introduce Malayalam into the liturgy and to cleanse the rite from 'hybridisms'.

The example of the local Jacobites and of the Malankarese is an encouragement to this, for they show a quite different practice. When, after the schism of 1653, the dissidents in Malabar had sought episcopal ordination for their leader from the Syrian Jacobite patriarch at Mardin in Mesopotamia, they came to adopt, not only the West Syrian rite, but also the Eastern practice of using the people's spoken language in public worship. Books have been printed by them in Syriac only—the Vatican Library has several examples—but they make extensive use of Malayalam, often to the almost entire exclusion of Syriac.

In 1930 a group of these Malabar Jacobites returned to Catholic communion, and were given the name of Malankarese (from the old name of Malabar) to distinguish them from their East Syrian fellows. They of course continued to use the West Syrian rite, and naturally kept their former ritual customs with it. Without having completely given up the Syriac language, they readily do everything in Malayalam, the use of which is optional, even for the words of eucharistic consecration. The rite remains substantially pure, with its own form of vestments and everyday sacerdotal dress, which have disappeared among the East Syrian Malabarese.

But the leader of the Malankara movement, the archbishop Mar Ivanios Panikkerveetil (d. 1953), a very able man, unfortunately was not wholly uninfluenced by the fallacious idea that 'to be a good Catholic one must be Latin'; and he introduced some unnecessary innovations, or allowed them to be introduced. They were welcomed by some of the clergy, especially younger priests trained under Western auspices; but others oppose them energetically. Rome has several times reproved such alterations; they scandalize the dissidents and discourage them from returning to unity, for it seems to them that the Holy See intends to westernize them altogether. They point to the Malabarese as proof, which makes it urgent that the unhappy work of the sixteenth-century Portuguese in this matter should be undone.

Degrees of Understanding

It is easy enough to say that in a general way the eucharistic Liturgy and sacred offices of the Eastern rites are celebrated in languages that the people understand, and that such a case as that of the Malabarese is only an exception. But there are others, due to various circumstances; and, even when the liturgical language is close to the spoken tongue, we need to know in what measure a liturgy is intelligible to people who have had at least a primary-school education, which is now so widely available. For if they understand little or not at all, our statement is misleading, and we are faced with a situation which is more or less like that of Western Catholics in relation to Latin. Actually, the degree of understanding of liturgical language in the East is very variable indeed, and each people must be considered separately.

Arabic-speakers.—I use this expression because none of the people who speak Arabic today were speaking it at the time when they first received Christianity. Both eastern and western Syrians spoke Syriac, and in towns near the Mediterranean,

Greek; but even on the outskirts of these towns the language was Syriac. There is plentiful evidence of this: it is enough to recall the sermon in which St. John Chrysostom laments that he does not know Syriac: that sermon was preached at Antioch.[11] Both Greek and Syriac were used in public worship. Greek did not cease to be spoken till long after the Arab conquest, and in the Lebanon and elsewhere Syriac persisted till the end of the seventeenth century. Arabic began to appear in the liturgy of the Melkites in the eleventh century, and at first only for funerals and in the rubrics. In Egypt, the situation was similar, with Coptic and Greek; the former went completely out of common knowledge in the seventeenth century.

Arabic-speaking peoples understand whatever is said or sung in church in Arabic (that is, if their theological knowledge is equal to their language!). They understand nothing at all of whatever is in Syriac, though Arabic and Syriac belong to the same Semitic family (it must not be forgotten that the Maronites, and still more the other West Syrian Catholics, use a lot of Syriac). Around Tur-Abdin and the few other places where a simplified Syriac is still spoken, the most common liturgical prayers are easily understood.

There is a similar situation among the East Syrians or Chaldeans in Iraq. Here a considerable number of Christians speak Sureth, and their children learn Arabic at school. Sureth is not taught, but the clergy visit the schools to impart the elements of classical Syriac. It is only in the towns and wherever else Arabic influence is strong that the biblical lessons in the liturgy are read in Arabic. Sureth is in use even among those Chaldeans who live in Persia; Father Paul Bedjan, whose Syriac publications are well known to orientalists and who was a native of Persia, produced several religious books in Sureth for popular use.[12]

As for the Copts, a very great deal of their liturgy is in Arabic, and therefore presents no difficulty. Coptic and the surviving Greek elements are simply formal tongues unintelligible to nearly all the faithful.

Armenians.—There is a certain difference between classical and modern Armenian, but it is difficult to know how much. I believe that those Armenians who have kept their own speech can easily understand the usual prayers of the liturgy, but the rather numerous elements in verse are another matter. In any case, Armenians are so attached to their old language that it does not occur to them to ask for its modern form in church. However, those of Aleppo are an exception, as has already been indicated.

Greeks.—The Greeks, too, are extremely attached to their ancient national tongue, and one might therefore expect that they would understand all that is said in church: but it is not as easy as that.

There is a great gulf between the Greek of the Homeric poems and the speech of peasants in present-day Hellas; the language has evolved a very great deal, and it can be said that there are 'several Greeks'. After the Greek of the heroic age came that of the classics, which are still more or less thoroughly studied in secondary and higher education in Europe. In consequence of Alexander's conquests, this was somewhat simplified into the *koine glossa*, 'common speech'. Byzantine Greek more or less resembled this, with great variation among writers, some of whom were servile imitators of classical models. Lastly, there is what is called modern Greek, with a very simplified grammar, strewn with local idioms, and even with Turkish words among those who come from there. But in this modern Greek we have to distinguish between the tongue of polite society and that of lesser people, between the written and the spoken word. The man who thinks he knows modern Greek simply because he can easily read an Athens newspaper is greatly mistaken, as he finds out the first time he speaks to someone in the street. It is rather like the difference between 'standard' Italian and its local dialects, which number some fifty and sometimes even have their own little literature.

Well-educated Greeks readily speak what is called the 'purified' language, especially with foreigners who claim to know modern Greek; but in their homes and in daily life it is another matter: they then use an idiom that no barrister uses in court, no preacher in the pulpit, nobody making a formal speech—while if anyone used it in parliament there would be a scene. The grammar and vocabulary of this current speech are quite different, but its use is by no means considered to show lack of education. Apart from some popular novels, the Greek written in books and periodicals is still more variable: each writer makes his own language, more or less modelled on the old 'common speech' or even on the classics. The Greek of everyday conversation is not lacking in dignity and worth; many people prefer it to the 'purified' tongue, which is highly artificial, and would like to see it become the literary language; but those who are fiercely opposed to this are equally numerous.

Fundamentally, the Greek of the liturgy is the 'common speech' as it was in the third–sixth centuries, grammatically correct and very simple in style in the prayers. In the poetical part, on the other hand, that of the numerous *troparia* of the *kanones* and *stikhera*,[13] it is rather more difficult, but still clear unless the theological ideas complicate it. There are some pieces, happily few, of such a pedantic literariness that even experts in the language are daunted.[14]

Provided they have had some schooling, however little, it may be said that the people have no difficulty in understanding the language of the eucharistic Liturgy, the prayers of the Ritual, the most frequently repeated *troparia* (which are often known by heart), the gospels, and those parts of the epistles that are not too compressed or theological and do not deal with matters that today interest only specialists in dogma. There is no need for books, and there are only a few for the people, such as the *Synopsis*, containing the more common prayers, or Holy Week manuals. Some fifty years ago a publisher at Constantinople issued, under the title of *Synekdemos*, a sort of Mass and Office book for the laity; it was reprinted at Athens, but it was not a success.

There are adequate versions in modern Greek of the New Testament, and of the Old too (these last the work of the British and Foreign Bible Society),[15] and enthusiasts for wholly popular Greek have produced a version of the gospels in that idiom. But these innovations have had a rather warm reception, and any attempt to introduce that kind of Greek into church services would raise a storm worse than that caused by the adoption of the Gregorian calendar for fixed feasts (this led to serious trouble that is hardly composed yet). Greeks do not feel any need for a living language in public worship, and look on any translation as a sacrilege.

Slavs.—The question is still more complicated for the Slavs, whose present languages differ from one another and are unequally distant from the Staroslav of ecclesiastical use. So each people must be considered separately.

Russian is the nearest tongue to Staroslav, and a Russian of ordinary education easily follows the most common parts of the eucharistic Liturgy. But there are some expressions and constructions that elude him, and before the revolution of 1917 there were pamphlets available in which the more difficult of these, arranged in alphabetical order, were explained in current terms. It is certain that much of the Divine Office is beyond the comprehension of anyone who has not learned something of Staroslav. The translation of the Greek is too literal, and this servility sometimes makes nonsense of the text. Here and there a better translation is given in a footnote, but nobody had dared to correct the text itself; however, just before the revolution the Moscow books were revised with the object of giving a better and more comprehensible rendering of the Greek. In the editions published by the Eastern Congregation at Rome these corrections and improvements have been made in the text itself wherever it was clearly desirable. The position may be summed up in the words of Anatole Leroy-Beaulieu: 'In the sacred tongue, the people's piety finds a language sufficiently like their own to mean something, and sufficiently different and archaic to add solemnity to divine worship.'[16]

Ukrainian does not differ greatly from Russian, and the position is the same. Before their fine press was confiscated by the Soviet government, which pulped their stock of books to make paper for communist propaganda, the Catholic Basilian monks of Zovkva published several editions of a book of the principal liturgical offices, in which the rubrics are in Ukrainian but the text in Staroslav only. This was for the use of the people, who are extremely fond of singing in church. They certainly do not understand all they sing and hear; but they grasp the meaning of the parts most often used, and have some idea of the general sense of the rest.

Although Staroslav is simply old Bulgarian, modern Bulgarian is further away from it than Russian and Ukrainian. As well as differences in vocabulary, it has lost the numerous inflections of the declensions; and it has introduced an article at the end of substantives, borrowed from the Latin *iste, ista, istud*. This does not exist in Staroslav, Russian or Serbian; the innovation may have come through Rumanian, which has a final article copied from Latin *ille, illa, illud*. The Bulgars naturally pick up the meaning of what is most often said or sung in church, but that is as far as it goes; they understand little or nothing of the prayers of the Ritual, still less of the Divine Office. In the edition of the *Sluzebnik* published by the Bulgarian synod in 1924, the rubrics and explanations are given in Bulgarian, which does not say much for the learning of the clergy. The difference between Staroslav and Bulgarian can be studied in the *Trebnik* (Ritual) that appeared at Sofia in 1929: here the prayers, lessons and psalms are in both languages, one printed after the other; hymns and litanies are in Staroslav only, but the rubrics are again in Bulgarian.

Serbian is farther away still from Staroslav. At the most, the people grasp the general sense of what they hear most often; of the rest they understand nothing more than isolated words here and there. In 1887, and again in 1905, the Serbs of the diocese of Temesvar asked for the vernacular in their liturgy, but nothing came of it.

Georgians.—Their ancient Caucasian tongue has not developed much through the centuries; it follows that the people understand the meaning of all or nearly all of the text of their services, at any rate those of them who have been to a primary school.

Rumanians.—It goes without saying that the Rumanians can follow the meaning of all their services, since their liturgical language is their daily speech. The same is of course true of the Byzantine *Hungarians.*

Ethiopians.—Ge'ez, the original language of Ethiopia in which Christian worship is conducted, is understood only by those who have made a special study of it. It is the ancestor of three other tongues, of which Tigré and Tigrinya[17] are spoken in the former Italian colony of Eritrea. The third, Amharic, is further removed from Ge'ez than these, but it is now the official language of the country.

The people are much given to singing in church, though they understand practically nothing of what they sing. Accordingly, those Protestant missionaries who see the Eucharist only as a means of instruction want the Ethiopians to get rid of Ge'ez. This leads to complications. Italy, the country that launched an unscrupulous war of aggression against Ethiopia in 1935, is an officially Catholic nation; England, that gave shelter to the *negus*[18] and eventually drove the Italians out, is reputed to be exclusively Protestant. So, the simple Ethiopian argues, the Catholics invaded us, the Protestants rescued us. But the Ethiopian would not change his religious language for anything, however meaningless it is to him: Ge'ez is part of his national heritage. In 1926 the *negus* Haile Selassie was responsible for the publication at Addis Ababa of a handsome *Mashafa qeddâsê* (Book of Liturgies), containing the fourteen eucharistic anaphoras in use; an Amharic translation and explanatory notes were included, but the book was intended only for study, not for use in church.

Albanians.—There is every reason to believe that Bishop Fan Noli's translations are appreciated in Albania, where the language is taught in all primary schools, but Greek in the liturgy is far from having been superseded entirely. In southern Italy and Sicily, however, Albanian is no more than a household speech; its vocabulary is limited to the needs of pastoral and agricultural life, and of folk poetry, which is transmitted orally and often improvised. It is an impoverished tongue,

E

which even in Albania itself has had to borrow many words
from Greek and Italian.

Not till lately have the Italo-Albanians had a people's
prayer-book in which the Greek is printed in roman characters
with the Albanian version opposite. In Calabria at any rate,
church services are pretty well reduced to the eucharistic
Liturgy and evening Benediction, celebrated wholly in Greek,
which is quite unintelligible to the laity. In Sicily, as I have
said already, a very little Albanian can be heard in church.
Here and there a priest succeeds in singing a shortened Vespers
with his flock in Greek, but the text has to be transliterated into
roman letters, which does nothing to help understanding. The
trouble is that Albanian is not taught anywhere. People have
got used to this passive assistance at worship; and if ever the
use of a living language is seriously mooted, that language will
have to be Italian, which nearly all Italo-Albanians can now
understand. There is no other way out, but the clergy do not
yet see it.

To sum up. Among Arabic-speakers, the Melkites alone
understand all that is said in church, and the Copts for those
services that are all in Arabic. Maronites and other West
Syrians understand the more or less considerable parts that are
in Arabic, and the Malankarese all their Malayalam. The
Chaldeans grasp at least the general sense. Rumanians, Hungarians, Georgians and Albanians in Albania understand everything. So can Greeks in principle, but in fact it depends on the
individual's degree of education. Russians and Ukrainians can
follow those parts that are of frequent occurrence, but the rest
not always or even at all; the same may be said of Armenians.
Only the most ordinary formulas are intelligible to Bulgars
and Serbs. The Ethiopians, Italo-Albanians and Malabarese
do not understand the words of their services at all.

*   *   *

As a general rule Christians of Eastern rite, Catholic or not,
men or women, do not take a book with them to church.
There are small prayer-books, especially among the Catholics,

but nothing or almost nothing corresponding to the Missals and Vesperals that are more and more used in the Western church; some exception must be made for the Ukrainians and Ruthenians[19] and one or two Greek books. But generally speaking there is nothing more than such booklets as those for Holy Week or for the twelve gospel-readings of the Passion on Holy Thursday evening. Those who do not understand what they hear can but take part passively and very few complain of this, especially among the simple folk.

The Bilingual System

To complete this part, a few words must be added about the bilingual system and how it is practised.

Normally in the Christian East each ethnical element has one liturgical language. Sometimes this language has been changed in the course of history: and sometimes one tongue has gradually taken the place of another, without the first going entirely out of use. Thus we get the bilingual system (in the case of the Copts, trilingual). There is nothing of the sort in the Western church,[20] except among the Glagolitic Slavs of Dalmatia, who are referred to in the chapter that follows. For them, the usage is carefully regulated: it is a local privilege, not personal; if the priest of a Glagolitic parish celebrates in a Latin church, he must do so in Latin. It is the same with the few local rites that still survive in the West: a Mozarabic priest may use his rite only in the special chapel at Toledo, an Ambrosian priest only in the diocese of Milan and a few other places that were once part of it; a Lyons priest who celebrates in a church of Roman rite must use that rite and also its calendar. Only the members of certain religious orders, *e.g.*, Carthusians, Dominicans, Carmelites, are allowed to use their proper rite in other churches. In the West, rite and language are local affairs; in the East, they are personal: the Eastern priest must keep to his rite wherever he is.[21]

The Glagolitic priest celebrating in Slavonic must use only that language: he is forbidden to say parts of the Mass in Latin, much more to do that at his own sweet will. A Melkite, on the contrary, being of Byzantine rite, can say this part in Arabic, that part in Greek, just as he pleases. Provided it can be done without upsetting good order, he can, without any special faculty, concelebrate in a low voice or even celebrate alone in Rumanian or Staroslav. The Byzantine rite enjoys great freedom in this matter. In a concelebration, each priest can choose either to keep to his own language, even in the parts he says aloud, or to conform to that of the majority: only the words of consecration must be said in a uniform tongue. In the days when Russian pilgrims used to flock to Jerusalem, I have heard the Greek deacon in the church of the Holy Sepulchre chant the long litany of the Liturgy in Greek, the first short litany in Arabic, and the second in Staroslav. In Bukovina I have heard a similar mixing of Staroslav and Rumanian. This was forbidden in Bessarabia when it was under Russian rule, but the prohibition was solely an example of using the Church for a political end, namely, the russification of Bessarabia: tyrannously enough, for the inhabitants were Ukrainian and Rumanian. It is quite possible that the Rumanians acted similarly when they regained possession of the province; certainly in Chisinau (Kishinev), its capital, I heard nothing but Rumanian.

Among the Catholic West Syrians and Maronites, the Antiochene rite is more strict, due to the influence both of conservatism and of the Council of Trent, as has been explained. Certain things may be said in Arabic alone, and these are carefully indicated in the books; but the Syriac of them is also given, and the celebrant is at liberty to use this if he pleases. The dissident Jacobites, on the other hand, make no difficulty about introducing other languages, and sometimes even translate as they go along. The Catholic Malankarese use Syriac or Malayalam indifferently at will.

The Chaldean rite is stricter still. In churches where the congregation knows only Arabic, the scriptural lessons may be read in that tongue instead of Syriac; but that is about all.[22]

In the Alexandrian rite, Coptic, Arabic and Greek are freely used together, but there is very little in Greek.

Bilingualism in the strict sense is at present unknown to the Armenians, the Ethiopians and the Malabarese.

We find, then, that on this point as on many others, the discipline of the East is wider than that of the West, and it seems unquestionably to be better adapted to people's needs. It has another advantage, and not the least of several, which cannot be overlooked. For a long time now the West has been inundated by what are called popular devotions, a less desirable effect of which has been to help put the people further out of touch with the Church's public worship; the liturgy has gradually come to be regarded as a sort of speciality for the clergy. But the East has not experienced a need for such devotions; there all worship in church takes a liturgical form, and if it be desired to adopt some more recent practice, this ought to be done in a manner and with observances conformable to the liturgical usages of the place.[23] This is now being more and more clearly recognized. But it must be admitted that in times not long past Catholics often ignored it, and brought about a state of things that is in need of reform.

Here then I conclude this first part of my undertaking. We can now go on to the second, and consider what has been the attitude of the West, in particular of its highest ecclesiastical authority, to the use of living tongues in public worship.

2

THE WEST

CHAPTER ONE

SLAVONIC IN THE WEST

IT is natural enough that the first attempt in the West in later times to use the people's tongue in public worship should have been the work of two Easterners, St Cyril and St Methodius, apostles of the Slavs.

During the ninth century, a new field was open to Byzantine missionaries. Moravia, a country to the south of the Silesia of today and bordering on Germanic territory, had already been touched by Christianity, but the faith had been imposed rather than preached and taught. The German prelates of those days were rough warriors, and they showed it. The Moravian king, Rostislav, was baptized, but his people were frightened by the brutality of the Germans and did not follow his example. The ruler of the Bulgars, Boris, was still wavering between Rome and Constantinople, and Rostislav, profiting by his good relations with this neighbouring prince, addressed himself to the Byzantine emperor, Michael III, and asked for missionaries from him. This was the origin of the mission among the Moravians of the two brothers, Cyril and Methodius.

Cyril (baptized Constantine) was already a priest, but Methodius was probably then simply a monk, after a secular career in which he had been governor of one of the Slav regions which were then so numerous in the Eastern empire. The brothers had already been sent on a mission among the Khazars, a Slavonic-speaking Scythian people north of the Black Sea, where there was much Jewish religious activity; and they had been successful in converting these allies of Constantinople. Both of them knew at least one Slavonic dialect, and so were well qualified for their new mission. The

two brothers arrived in Moravia a little before 864. They
found a people who were completely illiterate, but they were
well-disposed, their king was already a Christian, and the
mission was soon prospering.

Moravian priests had to be trained and ordained, and for
that purpose it was necessary to give them some rudiments
of culture and to translate at least the Gospels and some
liturgical formulas into their language. St. Cyril composed an
alphabet, a rather complicated one, capable of expressing all
the sounds of the Slavonic that the Moravians spoke, and it is
this that is known as Glagolitic.[1] Cyril and Methodius being
Byzantines by birth and upbringing, it was natural that they
should give the liturgy of Constantinople to their neophytes,
and this is very probably what they did at first. But there were
already Christians in Moravia, baptized by the Germans, with
some priests; moreover, Rostislav was a vassal of the Western
emperor, and this vassalage could easily one day become
subjection pure and simple. St. Methodius was determined
not to have recourse to the encroaching Germans; he was some
years older than his brother and more of a statesman, and he
appears to have had an inspired idea.

Methodius knew that curious eucharistic rite called the
Liturgy of St. Peter, composed we know not where, but
perhaps in southern Italy, which has had a strange fortune. It
is simply a shortened form of the Liturgy of St John Chrysostom into which have been inserted prayers translated literally
from the Roman Mass, principally in the anaphora or canon.
The numerous variants in the manuscripts show that it was
not just a literary exercise but a liturgy that was really
used. It is this that Cyril and Methodius seem to have
translated from Greek into Slavonic, together with parts of
the Bible, and have then celebrated in Rome and there
gained the approval of Pope Adrian II for it; at the same
time, or perhaps later, they will have translated the three
Byzantine Liturgies and parts of other ecclesiastical books.
Later still, their disciples continued the work of translation
in Bulgaria, after they had been driven out of Moravia. It

was an application in the West of the Eastern principle of a people's language being at the same time their language of public worship.

The text of the seven Glagolitic leaves bought in Jerusalem by the Archimandrite Antoninus, head of the Russian mission there, and deposited by him at the theological academy of Kiev in 1874, in fact goes back to the ninth century, and is therefore contemporary with the first apostles of the Slavs. How those leaves got to Jerusalem it is impossible to say; but nobody now doubts that the 'Kievan fragments', as they are called, are the oldest relics of the Roman liturgy in Slavonic. In addition to other prayers of Roman origin, they contain the proper of the Mass of Pope St Clement I, who died in exile in the Khazar country and whose relics St Cyril found there.[2]

There are three existing recensions of the Greek Liturgy of St. Peter, those of Grottaferrata, near Rome, of Rossano in Calabria, and of Mount Athos in Macedonia, the last with two translations, into Gerogian and into Staroslav. Furthermore, we read in the Slav Life of St Methodius that one St Peter's Day Methodius celebrated, for Rostislav's nephew, Svatopluk, and his army, the Liturgy of St Peter in Slavonic. This Greek Liturgy, together with the Byzantine Liturgies, must have been in use in eastern Illyricum, which comprised almost the whole of the Balkan peninsula and until 732 belonged to the Roman patriarchate, with Thessalonika as its capital. The Latin prototype of the Slavonic version is not the Roman canon of the ninth century, but of the earlier Gregorian Sacramentary;[3] the three older Croat Glagolitic missals have the same dependence. The ninth-century Slavonic Eukhologion of Sinai, which shows linguistic peculiarities which may be called 'Bohemianisms', also contains elements derived from the Roman liturgy. It would follow then that St Cyril and St Methodius did not translate the Roman canon from manuscripts of the ninth century but from a Greek text which depended on a Latin archetype of the late seventh. In any case, their work will have been twofold, partly in respect of

the Byzantine liturgy and partly of the Roman; but its precise
extent is impossible to determine.[4]

★   ★   ★

When their first candidates were sufficiently prepared, Cyril
and Methodius had to think about getting them ordained. In
Rome or in Constantinople? According to Slavonic sources,
they decided on Rome. Anyway, we find them in 867 at
Venice, which was on their shortest route to either Rome or
Constantinople. There they were involved in a dispute with
the Venetian clergy, who maintained that there were only
three languages which could be used in divine worship:
Hebrew, Greek and Latin. Did Pope St Nicholas I get wind
of this and, in view of his troubles with the Patriarch Photius
over Bulgaria, want to remind these missionaries that Moravia
was part of the patriarchate of Rome and not of Constantinople? It is not known; but the pope invited them to visit
him. Death took him almost at once, and it was his successor,
Adrian II, who welcomed the brothers. They celebrated in
his presence and in various other churches, and the liturgy in
Slavonic was approved by the pope, who had the best qualified
of the Moravians ordained to the priesthood; the others
received the diaconate. It was a great success, but St Cyril did
not enjoy it for long. His health was very bad, and he retired
to a small Byzantine monastery near the present church of
St Praxedes; here he died, on 14 February 869. Contrary to the
statement in the fifth lesson at Matins in the Roman Breviary
on 7 July, Cyril does not seem to have been made bishop; but
Methodius was, as archbishop of Pannonia with jurisdiction
over Moravia.

Methodius returned to Moravia early in the following year,
but soon fell a victim to the machinations of Svatopluk, who
had betrayed his uncle Rostislav to the Germans. Methodius
and the Greek monks he had brought with him were cast
into prison under the roughest conditions, where he remained for nearly three years. Rome knew nothing of
what was going on, till one of Methodius's companions

escaped and informed Pope John VIII, who had succeeded Adrian II in 872.

At the beginning of his pontificate, John VIII shared the opinion of those who claimed that Greek and Latin were the only languages fit to be used in divine worship. (He could not have been aware of what was happening in Eastern lands under the Arabs, for since the Moslem conquest communications were practically impossible, in addition to which the Armenians, the Copts and a great part of the Syrians were in schism and heresy.) Accordingly, he forbade the liturgical use of Slavonic. But he was a great upholder of justice and right, and he insisted that St Methodius be restored to his see, and later reserved to himself judgement on Methodius when he was accused. For Methodius was convinced that to abandon the use of Slavonic would be to give the signal for the return of the Germans and the undoing of all his work; he therefore did not feel bound to observe the pope's direction about Slavonic and continued to celebrate in the language that the Moravians understood. And, as a Byzantine, he did not add the words 'and the Son' (*Filioque*) to the Creed. That was quite enough to enable his enemies to charge him with heresy, and in 879 he was summoned to Rome.

Methodius had no difficulty in clearing himself. John VIII declared his orthodoxy; moreover, he did not hesitate to reverse his former decision, and formally approved the liturgical use of Slavonic. But, at the request of Svatopluk, the pope consecrated a certain German, named Wiching, to be suffragan to Methodius. By so doing the pope had, all unknowingly, signed the death-warrant of St Methodius's work in Moravia. If this had not happened, it is possible that all the Slavs in the Western church today would have had the whole of their public worship in a partly intelligible language, for John VIII approved Slavonic, not merely for some prayers, but for all the Mass and Office. The East had always acted on the principle that one language is as good as another before God, and now the West had done so too. Nor was Methodius required to add 'and the Son' to the Creed, or to alter other

Byzantine customs, notably concerning fasting and abstinence, which he had thought it well to retain.

John VIII embodied his decisions in a letter to Svatopluk, which he handed to St Methodius for delivery. The pope did not give this letter to Methodius to read, but he explained the contents to him, and it ought to have been taken to Svatopluk immediately. But the Moravian prince was at that time adventuring abroad, now among the White Croats north of the Carpathians, now in the plains of Poland. Methodius, having had to make a long detour to avoid passing through German territory, was very tired; and so instead of delivering the letter at once, he waited till Svatopluk should return. Bishop Wiching, on the other hand, was quite at home in the lands of the German leaders, and he lost no time. He had brought with him from Rome (he had gone there with Methodius in 879) a forged papal letter, modelled on the real one, and in it was a reference to Methodius having made a vow at St. Peter's tomb that he would not use Slavonic when celebrating the Mysteries. Svatopluk, like many primitive people, had superstitious reverence for a vow—he who swore the most impressively was in the right. Wiching knew this, and was calculating on it.

Pope John VIII was convinced that to maintain the faith of the young Moravian church it was necessary at all costs to keep St Methodius at its head. But he was in a difficult position at that time in relation to his own *curia*, to a good part of the Roman clergy and to some of the laity. He had just recognized Photius as patriarch of Constantinople, and was negotiating with the Byzantine emperor for help against the incursions of the Saracens from Sicily. So it was said he was under the tyrannical influence of the Greeks. He had not been insistent with Methodius in the matter of the *Filioque* clause; but then the Roman church had not yet accepted it officially. On no other matter had there been any question of Methodius's orthodoxy, and if the pope had ever to call a council in his regard, no question of dogma would be involved; John was at ease on that score. But he feared opposition in the field of discipline and worship: it would then be certainly brought against him that he had forbidden Slavonic one year, and allowed it the next. For this reason he had confined himself, as he said in a letter to Methodius, to giving him his decisions by word of mouth, at the same time assuring him that they were repeated in writing in the letter to Svatopluk, as indeed they were.

It has been stated above that Wiching carried a false letter concerning Methodius. The two documents, true and false, were expressed in similar terms, but contradicted one another at crucial points: where John VIII's letter authorized the use of Slavonic, the forgery prohibited it absolutely; and Wiching was represented as being made independent of Methodius's jurisdiction, and himself responsible for the carrying-out of the pope's instructions. Svatopluk was more used to handling a sword than to appraising documents, and when he was confronted by the two letters he fell into the trap and rejected the true one.

The resulting vexations at first discouraged Methodius, but during the hard winter of 880–881 he wrote a long letter to Pope John VIII; this letter is not extant, but its terms can be divined from the pope's prompt reply at the end of March 881. At this moment John's political situation was still worse: he had crowned Charles the Fat as emperor, though he did not really want to; he had had to justify his policy towards the Greeks publicly before the new emperor in St Peter's basilica; and he was surrounded by partisans of Charles, who were openly opposed to himself. But John was not intimidated, and his reply to Methodius, though guarded in expression, was perfectly clear to anyone who had read or knew the contents of his real letter to Svatopluk. The liturgy in Slavonic was confirmed, but in general terms; Wiching was not expressly named, but was pointed to in words that could not be misunderstood; the story of the vow at St Peter's tomb was cautiously but formally denied. Methodius had told the pope that he was planning a visit to Constantinople in quest of help, and this too was approved by inference.

This letter from Pope John reached Moravia towards the end of April 881. Methodius communicated it to one of those gatherings of Slav warriors which were so common at this time, and it was received with every mark of respect. Wiching was repudiated by Svatopluk and excommunicated by Methodius, and he had to flee, probably to his protector and friend, King Arnolf, in Carinthia.

The four years that followed were uneventful for St Methodius and his enterprises, but things happened that would lead to their destruction when it was least expected. Svatopluk embroiled himself with the Emperor Charles, invading German territory, burning and harrying everywhere; then, with an about-turn characteristic of his adventurous impetuosity and untutored mind, he offered the fealty to the emperor that he had formerly given to the pope. St Methodius ended his earthly life in peace on 6 April 885, at Velehrad in Moravia, where his tomb became a place of pilgrimage, as it still is. Pope John VIII had preceded him by two and a half years, so that both were spared the sight of the ruins of their common work. John was followed by two very short pontificates, and then, in 885, Stephen V was elected.[5] Circumstances were such that this pope came to adopt a line of conduct in regard to the liturgy in Slavonic diametrically opposed to that of John VIII, believing, in complete good faith, that he was in fact following his predecessor's example.

Immediately John VIII died there was a violent reaction against certain aspects of his internal and external policies; it was the beginning of that sad period in the history of the Roman church which is called the 'iron century'. All the adversaries of the dead pope returned to favour, including some who, because of the offices they held, had easy access to the papal archives. Now in 876 John VIII, in circumstances that historians have not completely elucidated, had undertaken an extensive 'purge' of the most important men of the pontifical court; dignitaries who had hitherto been his advisers and recipients of his favour were condemned, excommunicated, sentenced to banishment for life. The storm-centre was the

bishop of Porto, Formosus.[6] We know the verdicts that were
pronounced against the accused, not from John VIII's official
regesta[7] (why, we are about to see), but from the dispatches
about them that were sent to leading persons of the Christian
world. The charges alleged were of the deepest gravity:
perjury, adultery, murder by dagger and poison, for example;
it could therefore be foreseen that those incriminated would
not miss any opportunity that might occur of getting rid of
compromising records. The death of John VIII provided that
opportunity. All the documents relating to the period 1 September 875 to 31 August 876 were torn from the *regesta*,
and the succeeding parts carried off to the monastery of Monte
Cassino. Now the parts thus stolen from the archives contained
those letters of John VIII that authorized the Slavonic liturgy;
the preceding letters that condemned it remained in Rome. It
was a matter that had no interest for the partisans of the bishop
of Porto.

Pope Stephen V was an energetic Roman of the old style,
but he had been kept out of things during John VIII's pontificate. Of those who could have given him exact information
about what had taken place, some were dead, while others
he had himself excluded from the *curia* immediately after his
election. The papal librarian from 879 had been Zachary of
Anagni, but he is not heard of after 883; he may have been
dead, or more probably he had retired to his bishopric of
Anagni, not wanting to come into collision with John VIII's
opponents when they returned to favour.

Wiching, reconciled with Svatopluk, could now return to
his attack on the work of St Methodius, in the persons of his
followers. By the end of 885 he was in Rome, bringing his
false letter with him. He soon learned that the part of John
VIII's *regesta* that compromised himself was no longer available; if Pope Stephen wanted to ascertain exactly what his
predecessor had decided about the liturgy in Slavonic, he
would find only its original condemnation in the *regesta*.
Wiching boldly produced his forgery, and had no difficulty in
getting it confirmed; it would now be no less easy to restore

German ecclesiastical influence in Moravia. He returned then, and was followed by a papal delegation to Svatopluk; the Slav party was defeated.

By the end of two years, most of Methodius's followers had taken refuge in Bulgaria. Here, by a simple adaptation of eight-century Greek uncials, they worked out a new alphabet for Slavonic, and used it in their translations of the Byzantine service books. It is this alphabet that nowadays is called Cyrillic, wrongly, for St Cyril did not make it; Cyril's real alphabet is the Glagolitic, which survived only in Dalmatia, where some of the followers of St Methodius settled down. Later on, the composition of Glagolitic was attributed to St Jerome, who was a native of Dalmatia, and this false attribution did not a little to keep it alive. Thus it came about that the Roman Mass is still celebrated in the Slavonic tongue in many of the parishes and coastal islands of Dalmatia.

During the pontificate of John IX, 898–900, there was some talk of restoring at any rate ecclesiastical self-government to Moravia, by giving it a hierarchy independent of the German bishops; but it was too late. While negotiations were in progress, the Hungarians invaded central Europe and, as a separate state, Moravia disappeared.

*   *   *

It was not till the later part of the nineteenth century that the various episodes of this strange story were pieced together.

When Wiching was in Rome with St Methodius in 880 and suspected that John VIII's decision would be favourable to Methodius, how did he find out the terms of the papal letter to Svatopluk? He could not see the letter itself, for the pope did not show it even to Methodius but simply communicated its contents; but there still remained the draft of the letter. To see that, it was necessary to win over one of the papal notaries, whose duty it was to draw up the acts of the Holy See, forward them to their destination, and transcribe them, either at once or at leisure, from the drafts into the official *regesta* of the pontificate. These notaries were not necessarily all trustworthy and honest men, especially in the Rome of that era. It has been noticed that Pope Stephen V's letters about German affairs are all in the hand of a notary named Gregory, which has raised the suspicion that it was very probably he who allowed himself to be bribed to communicate to Wiching the draft of John VIII's letter that he wanted to see.

We already know how Wiching altered the terms of this letter for the purposes of his forgery; where the pope praised Methodius, approved the use of Slavonic, and entrusted the carrying-out of the papal decisions to the archbishop, Wiching made the letter praise himself, forbid Slavonic, and make him independent of Methodius, with the duty of executing the pope's orders. These are just the things that Stephen V says in his letter to Svatopluk, deceived as this pope was by Wiching's forgery. For all the transpositions of words, use of synonyms and commonplace amplifications, the general lines and characteristics of the text used are retained. At only one point do an inversion of sentences and a wrong synonym betray the forger; but, had the authentic *regesta*, or rather a faithful copy of it, never returned to the papal archives, the solving of the problem would have been a very difficult matter.[8]

The part of John VIII's *regesta* stolen from the archives was taken to the abbey of Monte Cassino, after the pages compromising for certain members of the Formosan party had been torn out and destroyed. Why was the rest kept and lodged in a place of safety at some distance from Rome? Father Lapôtre suggests, with considerable likelihood, that it was because Formosus of Porto, who was ambitious to be pope one day, wanted to keep intact everything that bore on the schism of the patriarch of Constantinople, Photius; later on he was to treat Photius as severely as John VIII had treated him with respect and patience.

Why Monte Cassino was chosen is not known, and by the later part of the eleventh century the monks there themselves had forgotten, or were not clear about, the circumstances in which they had come into possession of a very valuable document. It was one that was very difficult to read because of the ancient writing, and some words, especially proper names, were unintelligible; but they decided to have a copy made as faithfully as possible by their best scribes, who were not, however, successful in overcoming all the difficulties of their task. The original document has disappeared, when and how will probably never be known. About 1227 the building that housed the papal archives at Rome was destroyed by fire, and with it all its contents; that is why, for the centuries before Pope Innocent III (d. 1216), there remain only the dispatches that have since been retrieved from all over the place. But it was necessary to try to reconstitute the archives; and in circumstances that are not known, a canon of St Peter's, Berard, came into possession of the copy of the fragmentary *regesta* of John VIII made at Monte Cassino. Berard gave this to the pope, perhaps Clement IV (d. 1268), and it is still at the Vatican, where it is numbered I in the long series of registers of the Holy See. It contains John VIII's letters for the last six years, or rather, the last six indictions, of his pontificate, from 877 to 882.

It is, then, quite clear why Stephen V in 885 did not know that John VIII had given approval to Slavonic in the liturgy in 880, and therefore relied on the false letter produced by Wiching. The fact is that the first later pronouncement in favour of Slavonic was by Innocent IV in 1248, and this was given because at that time it was believed that the Slavonic liturgy was the work of St Jerome. The second was given by Clement VI in 1346, by which date the copy of John VIII's mutilated *regesta* had been deposited in the papal archives. Later on, Urban VIII and Innocent X were so well aware of John VIII's real decisions that they particularly referred to them. So in the long run Wiching failed to destroy the principle which Pope John enunciated in the following words:

There is nothing contrary to the faith or to sound doctrine in singing Mass in the said Slavonic language, or in reading the holy Gospel and the sacred lessons from the New and Old Testaments, properly translated and expressed, or in chanting other offices of the Hours in the same tongue.[9]

The pope could not have expressed his mind more clearly.

⋆ ⋆ ⋆

Nothing could be more complicated and inconsistent than the history of the Glagolitic Missal and Breviary, whose first elements we have shown to go back to SS. Cyril and Methodius, or at any rate to their time. When the Hungarian tempest had passed and King St Stephen (d. 1038) with his people had been converted to Christianity, the embryonic missal of which something has survived in the 'Kievan fragments' was gradually completed. Apparently this work was done by Benedictines in Bohemia, who had come from Dalmatia and established a monastery at Sazava, to the south of modern Pardubice. Nevertheless, in a letter addressed to King Vratislav of Bohemia in 1080, Pope St Gregory VII forbade the use of Slavonic, on the ground that were the Holy Scriptures available to all and sundry they would be wrongly interpreted.[10] The letter may however make an allusion to the work of Cyril and Methodius, for it goes on to say that what was allowed in earlier ages of the Church ceases to be allowed once Christianity has spread and the faith become well rooted. At this time of course John VIII's letter to Svatopluk was not available, and it is quite possible that Gregory VII was confusing the Slavs with the Arian Goths. Such mistakes were common in the middle ages: for a century and more after their conversion the Ruthenians, for example, were supposed to be still heathen; for they depended ecclesiastically on Constantinople and not directly on Rome, and consequently Rome did not know about them.

Pope Innocent IV, on the other hand, in 1248 authorized Slavonic in almost the same terms as John VIII;[11] he and his contemporaries believed that the Slav alphabet had been composed by St. Jerome, who was born at Stridon in Dalmatia. In 1346 Clement VI approved the foundation of the Benedictine monastery of Emaus, at the gates of Prague, and there the offices were celebrated in Slavonic. This monastery was brought to ruin during the troubles aroused by the heresy of John Hus, but it was restored in 1593 and continued to be peopled by Dalmatian monks with their Slavonic liturgy. However, they gradually died out during the following forty-two years, and were replaced by Spanish monks from Montserrat in Catalonia: that was the definitive end of liturgical Slavonic in Bohemia.

But though it disappeared in that country it was carried on in Dalmatia, but not without difficulties. The bad feeling between the Slavs of the countryside and the numerous Italians in the towns was of old standing. So early as the ninth century a council at Split (Spalato) had forbidden the ordination of priests who knew only Slavonic; a defender of the language, Bishop Gregory of Nin (Nona), appealed to Pope John X (d. c. 928), who first forbade it and then said he would think more about it: the upshot is not known. Under Alexander II (d. 1073), the use of Slavonic was again rejected: at that time there were those at Rome who regarded St Methodius as a heretic and the Slavs were confused with Arian Goths. We have just seen how another historical mistake contributed to Innocent IV's making a contrary decision. The use of Slavonic in public worship of the Western rite was not finally and definitively approved till 1631, by Urban VIII.

In 1648 Innocent X ordered a revision of the Slavonic or Glagolitic Breviary, and it was printed for the first time in 1688, at the Propaganda Press; there was a second edition during the eighteenth century. But this was the last; today the clergy say the Divine Office in Latin, though on the greater feasts Vespers and Compline are celebrated in Staroslav. Of the Missal, on the other hand, six printed editions are known up to that of 1896, and in these the Glagolitic alphabet continued to be used in spite of its complexity. Then the Dalmatian bishops decided that the Missal should undergo a new revision, from a linguistic point of view, in order to get rid of the Croatian and Ruthenian elements that had crept in at the hands of previous editors of those nationalities. This time the work was entrusted to a Slavonic scholar of European reputation, Dr Joseph Vajs, of Prague. The text was carefully emended, and this time printed in roman characters, with the addition of special signs designed to express all the sounds of the Slavonic. The book was very finely produced at the Vatican Press and was published in 1927, the whole edition being intended for Dalmatia.

This is the Missal that is now in use, in many parishes of the dioceses of Krk (Veglia), Senj (Segna), Zadar (Zara) and Split, and in the Dalmatian province of the third order regular of St Francis. Its use is governed by a decree of the Congregation of Sacred Rites of 5 August 1898: it is not a personal but a local privilege, belonging to those places where it has a prescription of at least thirty years; a list of such was to be drawn up, which was not to be altered; the only language used for Mass must be Staroslav; it must be printed in Glagolitic characters only (This rule has been superseded); if it is the people's usage to sing the responses and chants they must do so in Staroslav, but their texts may be printed in roman characters; a Ritual in the Slavonic language may be used, provided it has been examined and approved at Rome (*What* Slavonic language is here referred to we shall see in a moment). Very detailed regulations are laid down to ensure that, in every 'Staroslav church', solemn Mass shall always be celebrated in that tongue and the sacraments ministered according to the Slavonic Ritual. For private Mass and Office, every priest is free to use Latin if he wishes.

In 1935, the Holy See concluded a concordat with Yugoslavia, though it was never ratified by Belgrade. In this, Pope Pius XI confirmed the liturgical use of Slavonic to the degree and in the forms sanctioned by Leo XIII and Pius X; and it was declared that the Holy See 'was not opposed' to the

bishops being free to allow it 'in Slavonic-speaking parishes . . .
wherever the faithful unanimously desired it.'[12]

*   *   *

Of this 'Latin Slavism', if the expression may be allowed,
there is another matter which I am happy to be able to make
public, before turning to others which anyone can verify for
himself. My old colleague at the Vatican, Dr Ciro Giannelli,
has found, in a section of the libarary where no one would
think of looking for such a thing, a complete sixteenth-century
Missal in the Croat tongue as spoken at Dubrovnik (Ragusa);
this he has patiently deciphered and is preparing for publication. The successive 'layers' of the manuscript show that this
Missal, which was clearly intended for use in church, is in its
present form a partial copy of one more ancient. The introduction to Dr Giannelli's edition will certainly tell us more
about it; in the meantime we know for a fact that in the
fifteenth century, and perhaps earlier, an attempt was being
made to do for Croatia what St Cyril and St Methodius did
for Moravia.

The idea of liturgy in the spoken tongue had taken such a
hold on Slav minds that there was published in Rome in 1640
an integral version of the Roman Ritual in the 'Illyrian'
dialect, that is, in the common Croatian of Dalmatia. This
was printed by the Propaganda Press, and we learn from its
dedication to Urban VIII that that pope had ordered the book
to be published; it had the approbation of the vicegerent of
the Roman vicariate, of the deputy master of the Sacred
Apostolic Palace, and of the father general of the Society of
Jesus (at that time Muzio Vitelleschi), that is, of the highest
Roman authorities. The translator of this Ritual was Father
Bartholomew Kassić, S.J.,[13] himself a Dalmatian, and its object
was to remedy the ignorance of those clergy who had little
Latin, or none at all. Prayers, rubrics and everything else are in
Croat—there is not a single Latin word in the whole book. The
sung parts are given in plain-chant notation, and the chant
has undergone a certain amount of modification to adapt it to

Slavonic words. In his preface, Father Kassić relates the
difficulties he encountered in choosing a dialect that was widespread enough and understood by everybody concerned. The
original edition was reprinted as it stood at Venice in 1827; it
was corrected linguistically and republished at Rome in 1893,
and again at Zagreb in 1929. It is still in general use, though
the standard of education among the Dalmatian clergy is now
very different from what it used to be.

In 1932 the Congregation of Rites approved a similar Ritual
in Slovenian, in virtue of a grant by Pope Benedict XV in 1921.
I have before me an excerpt from this book, published at
Ljubljana in 1933 and entitled *Collection of Sacred Rites for the
Bishoprics of Lavant and Ljubljana*.[14] From this Ritual there is
derived another book, of a more general kind and this time in
the Dalmatian dialect: it contains the epistles and gospels for
Mass on Sundays and feasts, the sequences, and occasional
blessings, such as those of candles on 2 February and of ashes
on Ash Wednesday. It is called *Pisctole i evangelia*, a title that
needs no translation. I know of two editions: one printed by
the Propaganda Press at Rome in 1840, the other at Rjeka
(Fiume) in 1880.

The use of the living tongue, in a somewhat more limited
but still extensive form, spread from Dalmatia to all Croatian
regions. I have before me a Ritual printed at Graz in Austria
in 1887 by order of Archbishop Joseph Stadler of Sarajevo
and the bishops of his province.[15] The text is in Latin, but a
good part of the offices is given in Croat too: not only the rites
of baptism, marriage, and anointing of the sick, but also
communion outside of Mass, everything concerned with
ministering to the dying, the litany of the saints, certain
processions and prayers, as well as two observances borrowed
from the Eastern church, namely, the solemn blessing of water
on the eve of the Epiphany (this is also to be found in Germany)
and the announcing of the Resurrection on the night before
Easter. When I was travelling in Serbia in 1923–24 I was able
to find out for myself that the clergy of Roman rite there use
similar books when ministering the sacraments; and I have

been informed that the Czech clergy do the same in their own language.

There are, then, two groups of Slavonic liturgical translations at the present time. The first consists only of Staroslav or Old Slavonic, now simply a liturgical language; the second comprises the Dalmatian dialect, Croatian, Slovenian and Czech. These four are living tongues; but what is the significance for us of Staroslav, which is dead? Does not its use derogate from the principle of the legitimacy of using living languages in the Western liturgy, the principle recognized by Pope John VIII and confirmed by Urban VIII? Not at all: for at the time of St Cyril and St Methodius what we call Staroslav was very much alive. It was the language of those 'Slavdoms' of Thessalonika, over one of which Methodius had been governor for several years.

CHAPTER TWO

OTHER LANGUAGES IN THE WEST:
LATER DEVELOPMENTS

I N chronological order, the next translation of the Latin
Mass found after Slavonic was due to the efforts of the great
fourteenth-century Franciscan missionary, John of Monte
Corvino (d. 1328), who preached among the Mongols of
southern Siberia and converted their ruler, Kerguz (George).
Friar John had been preceded by Nestorian missionaries from
Persia and Mesopotamia, who were very active at this epoch,
before the almost complete destruction of their church at the
invasion by the Mongols after these had passed to Islam.
The Nestorian missionaries celebrated in Syriac; but this
language was completely unintelligible to the people, and
that in a region where frequent services were necessary,
since prayer was going on continually in the Buddhist
lamaseries.

The converted prince built a church for John of Monte
Corvino, who celebrated Mass therein according to the
Roman rite but in Uigur Turkish, which was the local
language. He planned to translate the whole of the Roman
offices, but this immense task was not completed: the prince
died, his brothers who succeeded him brought Friar John's
converts back to Nestorianism, and John made the imperial
capital, Peking itself, the centre of his mission. The use of
Uigur Turkish was evidently due to John of Monte Corvino's
own initiative, without recourse to Rome, with which
communication was all but impossible at that era; but the
happening is nevertheless very significant. The following is
the pertinent passage from the second of John's three extant
letters:[1]

I have an adequate knowledge of the Tartar language and writing, which is the usual language of the Tartars. I have now translated the whole New Testament and the Psalter into it, and had them written down in their beautiful characters. I testify, read and preach publicly, bearing witness to the law of Christ. I planned with the said King George, if he had lived, to translate the whole of the Latin office, so that it might be sung throughout the land where he held sway; and while he was alive I celebrated Mass in his church according to the Latin rite, in their language and using their script, including the words of the preface and canon.

Two Grants of Greek

At the end of the same fourteenth century we come upon Greek. Here it was not a question of the Liturgy of St Peter (the nature of which has already been explained in the previous chapter) but of the rite used by St Dominic's Order of Preachers. These friars had established themselves in the Pera quarter of Constantinople during the time of the Frankish emperors there, and spread from thence to other places. One of them, Friar Maximus, in 1398 obtained permission from Pope Boniface IX to translate the whole Dominican liturgy into Greek, and to make use of it. Only the pope's reply to the request has survived, but it is clear enough:[2]

It is your wish to celebrate Mass and the other sacred offices in public in the Greek tongue, in a clear voice, whether speaking, reading or singing. . . . Accordingly, we . . . being favourable to your requests in this matter, [grant] that, in Catholic churches and other places where you may happen to be for the time being in the said parts of Greece, you may celebrate Mass and the other sacred offices in the Greek language; and this in accordance with the rite and customs of the Order of Preachers . . . without any change of the meaning or significance of the words.

Whether Friar Maximus ever made his translation is not known;[3] but eight years later, on 19 February 1406, Pope Innocent VII issued a rescript in favour of the famous Greek

scholar of Constantinople, Manuel Chrysoloras: it enabled him
to receive holy orders (which in fact he did not do) and to
celebrate Mass, or have it celebrated for him, according to the
Dominican rite translated by him into Greek. Manuel
Chrysoloras was one of those Greeks who continued faithful
to the union that was effected at the Council of Lyons in 1274;
he even went to the length of forsaking the Byzantine for the
Roman rite, through the Dominicans at Constantinople with
whom he had very close contacts. He also translated a Mass
attributed to St Gregory the Great, and the blessings of candles,
ashes and palms from the Dominican rite. The text of his
petition to the Holy See has disappeared, as has that of
Innocent VII's indult; but there is a sufficiently detailed analysis
of it in one of the old inventories of the Vatican archives.
Manuel's other translations are in manuscripts of the Turin and
Venice libraries.

The Dominican Liturgy in Armenian

During the same fourteenth century a translation of the
Dominican Missal and Breviary was made into Armenian, and
this eventually received formal approbation, in the following
circumstances.

In the twelfth century the Friars Preachers became established in Cilicia, where the Armenians were in communion
with Rome following on the Crusades, and from thence they
penetrated into Armenia proper. In 1330 an archbishopric was
founded at Nakhichevan, near the Persian frontier north of
Lake Urmia. At this time there was no legislation about the
use of liturgical rites, and the friars thought out a special
system for their apostolic work, a system which unfortunately
came to be followed for several centuries.

Nowadays, after Leo XIII and Pius XI have vigorously
promoted the tentative efforts under Pius IX, it is taken for
granted that, so far from seeking to reconcile Eastern dissidents
to the Western rite, missioners should themselves pass to one
or other of the Eastern rites, whether for a time or definitively.

That is what is done today among the Melkites in Syria, the Copts in Egypt, and elsewhere; most of the priests trained at the *Russicum* in Rome, for work in Russia when that country shall again be open, are of Latin-rite origin. But the Dominicans of the middle ages in Armenia did not themselves adopt the Armenian rite; instead they translated their own liturgy into the Armenian language, and it was thus that Armenians whom they reconciled with the Catholic Church worshipped.

A special branch of the Order of Preachers was organized, under the name of Brothers of Unity, which produced both learned men and martyrs.[4] Theological works were translated into Armenian, as well as the Dominican Missal and Breviary. According to the historians of the order, these last were translated by the first archbishop of Nakhichevan, Bartholomew the Short of Bologna (d. 1333);[5] whether the work of him or of another, the version is certainly old, going back to the fourteenth century. These liturgical books were still in manuscript at the beginning of the eighteenth century, when the Congregation for the Spreading of the Faith submitted them for examination to the Holy Office. On 6 September 1713, they were approved for printing, 'praevia tamen recognitione, revisione et correctione facienda per D. Cacciadur de Arachel, et si ei contingerit aliquid dubium, S. Congregationem certioret'; this decision was confirmed by Pope Clement XI on the following day. Hachatur Arakhel, as his name is better spelt, had been a student at the Propaganda College and ministered to the Armenian colony in Venice. But his choice as reviser was perhaps not ideal, for among his fellow countrymen he had the reputation of being a poor linguist.[6] However, the Breviary was published by Antonio Bartoli at Venice in 1714. For the revision of the Missal, the Holy Office had appointed Abbot Peter Mekhitar of Sivas, founder of the monks called after him Mekhitarists, to assist Arakhel, and it at length came from the Propaganda Press at Rome in 1728; the notation of the chant was not given.

These books were used by the Brothers of Unity and their flock only till about the middle of the eighteenth century. By that time the faithful were reduced to a few thousand in number and, unable any longer to withstand Moslem pressure, they were dispersed; the most important group became absorbed in the Latin Catholic colony at Smyrna, where there still a few families descended from them. As for the books, are they are extremely rare, as may be imagined. In 1923 I was at Gherla in Transylvania, where there is a remnant of an Armenian colony that was once very flourishing. What was my astonishment to find a copy of this Dominican Missal in the Armenian church there, though the proper Armenian rite was in use therein: this Missal was being used for the reading of the epistles and gospels of the eucharistic Liturgy, in spite of the fact that its calendar was completely different!

The language of these books is literary Armenian, but at the relevant time the difference between the two idioms, classical and modern, was not yet so marked as it is today. It was, then, an example of the use of a living language in public worship, and moreover in a rite that is Western.

A 'Sacerdotal' in Albanian

There is in the Vatican Library (*Raccolta generale, Liturgia*, III, 194), a curious book that has hitherto escaped the notice of bibliographers: it is a unique copy of what was called a Sacerdotal, or Priest's Book, comprising extracts from the Missal and the Ritual. It is in Albanian, translated by a priest named Gjon Buzuku, and was printed in Rome in 1555; its condition shows that it was in use for a long time, but it carries no indication of official approval. It is, however, impossible to imagine such a book being published in Rome at that time without approbation, and approbation presupposes a concession.

The reason for this publication was certainly the lack of education of Albanian priests of Roman rite, who in those days no more understood Latin than did their Slav colleagues in Dalmatia. This ignorance is confirmed by another book, equally rare, in the same department of the Vatican Library

(V, 51). It is a Ritual, edited by Peter Budi, bishop of the Albanian diocese of Sappa, a see that still exists, and was published in Rome in 1621, Pope Gregory XV paying the cost. The text is wholly in Latin, but all the rubrics are in Albanian. This, however, would not be inconsistent with Albanian having been approved for use in public worship, probably by Paul III or Julius III.

The Council of Trent

In No. 11 of the *Maison-Dieu* series,[7] Canon A. G. Martimort contributes an article in the course of which he gives an excellent summary of what happened at the Council of Trent with regard to liturgical languages (pp. 47–50). There is no mystery about this, for the proceedings of the Council have been published in full; it is true that the five great volumes of the *Görresgesellschaft*, which paid for this monumental publication, are little known outside the ranks of the learned, but certainly some at least of the consultors of the second section of the Congregation of Sacred Rites, those who are concerned with the liturgy, are familiar with them. Those who require a quick reference will obviously turn to cap. viii of the Council's 22nd session, and the canon ix that follows it. The texts are well known: 'Although the Mass contains much teaching for the faithful people, it did not appear expedient to the Fathers that it should be celebrated all over the place [*passim*, says the very classical Latin] in the spoken tongue'. Then follows the direction to the clergy with cure of souls often (*frequenter*) to explain to the faithful, during Mass and either by themselves or through others, those things that are read threat: that is, not simply the gospel and even the epistle, but other things that are said and done. The pertinent canon condemns (*inter alia*) the Protestant principle: 'Should anyone say that . . . the Mass ought to be celebrated only in the spoken tongue . . . let him be condemned.'

As Canon Martimort points out, for Protestantism the Mass and the sacraments do not draw their value from the simple fact that the one is celebrated and the others ministered: 'their efficacy is simply that of a predication, and this preaching becomes entirely useless if the people do not understand it'. It was simply this that the Council meant to condemn.

Today the gospel reading is everywhere expounded, at any rate at the parish sung Mass, but what proportion of the people are there? How many of them are content with a low Mass? Surely these last are the great majority, and sometimes the whole of a congregation. It is almost unknown that the epistle should be commented on, while as for the other things that are said and done, and their meaning, it can be said that they are almost never referred to. This does much to explain the passive attitude, the simply 'being there', of so many men and women, the saying of the rosary (which can be done better at another time) or the reading from some little devotional book that has no direct bearing on what is going on at Mass. That is what happens very often indeed, at any rate in my experience, especially in Italy.

We ought, then, to examine the proceedings of the Council of Trent themselves, to see what the Fathers, or at any rate those who expressed their views, thought about celebration in a living tongue, apart from the matter of the efficaciousness of Mass and the sacraments in themselves. Canon Martimort did this in his article, but it will perhaps be useful to add a few details. [8]

The relevant *capitula* were first submitted to the Fathers in the form of articles, which were later put into the form of canons. The ninth of these condemns those who deny the legitimacy of speaking parts of the canon of the Mass, including the words of consecration, in a low voice, those who declare that Mass ought only (*tantum*) to be celebrated in the spoken tongue, and those who maintain that the mixing of a little water with the eucharistic wine is contrary to Christ's institution. The Fathers were unanimous on these points, but only one of them, the Spanish theologian Francis de Santis, presented the argument that the three languages represented on the title of Christ's cross, Hebrew, Greek and Latin, were the only ones worthy to be used in divine worship. He was certainly seven hundred years behind his time.[9]

The eighth *capitulum*, which precedes the canons, was put before the Fathers at the general assembly of 6 August 1562, the solemn sessions being reserved for definitive enactments. It was drawn up in a rather different way from what we now read, as quoted above. It ran:

> The Latin language, too, which is used for the celebration of Mass in the Western church, is in the highest degree appropriate, seeing that it is common to many nations. It seems beyond doubt that, were Mass to be carried out in each people's vulgar tongue, the divine Mysteries would be celebrated with less reverence. There would even be grave danger of various errors arising in many translations, with the result that the mysteries of our religion would seem to differ, instead of being, as they are, one and unchanging [*simplicia*, again in the classical sense].

The discussion went on through five assemblies, from 11 to 24 August. Five bishops spoke, and four of them were urgent that there should be no condemnation of the principle of celebrating in a living tongue. The bishop of Veglia (Krk), in whose diocese Slavonic was used as well as Latin, was even opposed to Latin, and he recalled that the eucharistic Liturgy is celebrated in every language in the church of the Holy Sepulchre at Jerusalem. The bishop of Saint Asaph in Wales observed that there are many things (*multa alia*) that ought to be understood by the people at Mass beside the gospel reading.[10] The sole person to express himself in favour of Latin exclusively was the bishop of Nîmes, a diocese where Protestants were, and still are, very numerous. Among the theologians who gave an opinion, Caesar de Ferrand cited a *novella* of Justinian, no. 137, in favour of living languages. I have had the curiosity to look up this text, for, though it would have been nothing out of the ordinary in the East, it would have been an early affirmation of its cherished principle from an oft-quoted juridical authority. And lucky it was that I did: for I found that Justinian was not talking about languages, living or dead, but was inveighing against the habit of certain bishops and priests of celebrating the Eucharist and conferring Baptism 'silently', that is to say, in so low a voice as to make their words almost unintelligible.[11]

The assembly then went on to discuss communion in both kinds for all, and the question of liturgical language dropped out of sight. On 5 September, the new version of cap. viii—that which we have today—was submitted to the Fathers, but nobody spoke again on the subject of Latin. In the study to which I have just referred (note 11), Father Schmidt writes:

> The reason Latin was retained was simply one of convenience and propriety. In the sixteenth century it was like a second mother-tongue, and the depository of all religious, scientific and cultural values; there was, too, the difficulty of translations. Were the Council to have decided for vernacular tongues, the change would have been an abrupt one, a forced measure not arising naturally from the circumstances. . . . Moreover, in view of Protestantism and its linguistic innovations, the introduction of vernacular languages into the liturgy might have been inter-preted as an approval of the Reform by following its example.[12]

To sum up: The Council of Trent did not absolutely reject the use of a living tongue in the celebration of the sacred Mysteries, and the virtual unanimity of those Fathers who gave reasons for their opinions was incompatible with a radical condemnation, as is clearly shown by the use of the word *tantum* (only) in canon ix. That might seem a small point, but it is in fact of capital importance. The Council simply answered: *Non expedire*, It is not expedient. But it does not follow that what was not expedient in the sixteenth century is not expedient in the twentieth.[13]

Georgian, Persian, Armenian and Arabic in the Roman Liturgy

This interpretation is confirmed by a decision of the Con-gregation for the Spreading of the Faith in 1631 with reference to Georgian. It was not a question of the Byzantine rite in Georgian—there would have been no difficulty about that— but of the Roman rite. The Theatine clerks regular had arrived in Georgia towards the end of 1628, and they soon found it would be a good thing if they were able to celebrate Mass in Georgian and Armenian. (In those days it did not occur to anyone that it would be more natural for them to adopt the Byzantine rite of the country; and perhaps the Holy See would have been opposed to it, in accordance with con- temporary opinions on the subject that were to subsist for a long time yet.) The request was duly examined in Rome; the resulting decision is a little long, but too important not to be given here in full:

> With regard to permission to celebrate Mass of the Latin rite in the Georgian or the Armenian language, the said Fathers [of the Congregation] unanimously agreed that this should not be granted at present, unless it would·be a powerful means for the reconciliation of the Georgians. One of the said Fathers pointed out that the Council of Trent presents no obstacle here, since it only forbade the celebration of Mass in the vernacular; he said further that that part of the Mass called 'of the learners,' being instructional, can be allowed to all peoples in their own tongue, if Latin or Greek be not in use among them. Another Father added that should the Georgians be willing to embrace the Latin rite, Mass in their own language ought certainly to be granted to them, for Latin or Greek are not known in their country and there would be no Georgian able to offer the sacrifice to God with knowledge and propriety.[14]

No Missal of the Roman rite in Georgian is known to be in existence, whether printed or manuscript.

A similar case had arisen seven years earlier, in 1624. The Carmelites in Persia had asked permission to celebrate Mass in Persian, and the matter was discussed by a full meeting of the Congregation for the Spreading of the Faith, at which Pope Urban VIII presided in person. The request was granted, on the conditions that the Roman rite should be adhered to, the translation should be approved in Rome, and only one Mass in Persian should be celebrated in one day in each particular church. In the event, it seems as if this translation was never made and used; but the principle of the concession remains.[15]

It is a curious thing that only three years later the same Carmelites sought authorization to celebrate also in Armenian, evidently for the large Armenian colony at Julfa in Persia, and that this time their request was refused, the reason given being that 'Concessions of this kind are a great hindrance to the communications of churches with the Roman church'.[16] This does not seem to be very convincing: the Congregation must have known the practice of the Dominican Brothers of Unity in Armenia, with whom it was in constant touch. I have tried to find the originals of these two requests, for Persian and Armenian; but the Congregation's archives for this period are classified according to an antiquated and very defective system which cannot now be changed, and to continue my search would entail much more time than I can spare, and without much hope of a successful result.

In 1757 the Holy Office had to pronounce on a custom of the Capuchin friars in Georgia. At a sung Mass, the celebrant first read the epistle and gospel in a low voice in Latin, and then chanted them in Georgian or Armenian. The Holy Office allowed this, on condition that the lessons were chanted in Latin before being chanted in the other language; provided, too, that the Georgian or Armenian used was the literary language, and a faithful version of the Vulgate or Greek biblical text.[17] (An analogous usage was likewise authorized for the eucharistic Liturgy of the Armenian rite in 1777: after the singing of the gospel in classical Armenian, it was repeated in Georgian by way of explanation. The Congregation regarded this Georgian reading as the exposition of the gospel which the Church requires.)[18]

The Capuchins of Akhaltsikhe pointed out that not only were the epistle and gospel of the Latin Mass repeated in Georgian, but the collects as well; so they asked that the same might be done for Armenians. A favourable reply was given in 1784.[19]

On the other hand, the Custody of the Holy Land reported in 1822 that it was there customary, at a Latin Mass, for the gospel to be read in Arabic, and for the server to repeat the *Gloria in excelsis*, the Creed, the *Suscipiat*, the *Sanctus* and the Lord's Prayer also in Arabic. The Congregation gave its decision in 1824. It was to the effect that the gospel could be read in Arabic before the sermon, as part of the preaching, but the other things were forbidden. However, three years later this decision was reversed in part: the Congregation conceded the reading of epistle and gospel in Arabic during the Mass itself, and not as part of the sermon, provided they were read in Latin first, this having been the custom in all local churches of Latin-rite clergy from time immemorial.[20]

Chinese

Canon Martimort records[21] that on 26 March 1615 the Holy Office, in the name of Pope Paul V, issued a decision favourable to celebration in Chinese by priests of that nationality. The Chinese, whose language is monosyllabic and has no sound corresponding to the letter *r*, often have much difficulty in learning and prouncing Latin; nevertheless they succeed so well in doing so, speaking and writing it quite fluently, that all their ecclesiastical education is carried out in Latin, like that of the Indo-Chinese. It is very likely that this seventeenth-century request was connected with the difficulty of Chinese for most European missionaries, because of its fine variations of pitch that are almost imperceptible to the non-Chinese ear. In any case, a translation of the Missal, delayed by persecutions, was eventually finished by Father Luigi Buglio, S.J., and was printed at Peking in 1670.[22] According to Sommervogel's bibliography of the writers of the Society of Jesus, Father Buglio also translated the Roman Breviary and a sort of Ritual into Chinese.

Unhappily, it was just at this time that there began among

missionaries the great controversy on the subject of what were
called the 'Chinese Rites', that is, certain observances in honour
of Confucius and of ancestors; today the Church has to a
considerable degree allowed these observances to Chinese
Christians, deciding that they are of a purely civil character,
like observances in honour of the Unknown Soldier in the
West. But in those days, when the theological controversies
of the sixteenth and seventeenth centuries about grace were
still heated, there was deep disagreement on the subject of these
Chinese Rites. Papal intervention failed to establish concord,
and even today, though the numerous relevant documents in
the archives of the Congregation for the Spreading of the
Faith can be consulted, their publication is strictly forbidden.

But in spite of all the difficulties Father Buglio's Chinese
Missal came into actual use, for there was a decree of the
Congregation in 1755 which prohibited that use and also
forbade chants and prayers in Chinese during Mass.[23] The
second part of this provision is no longer observed today, just
as a similar prohibition would be very difficult to enforce in
European countries. The times were not propitious for changes
of this kind, and so when Father Philip Couplet submitted the
Buglio Missal to the Congregation of Rites in 1680, he failed
to get approbation for it.[24] The suppression of the Society of
Jesus in 1773 and the subsequent era of revolution brought
disaster to the missions in China, which had to be re-estab-
lished on new foundations in the nineteenth century.

The language used by Father Buglio for the Missal was not
the common spoken Chinese, which varies from province to
province, but what is called Mandarin, the literary idiom of
classical writings. Was this distinction made in Rome? In any
case the encouraging attitude towards Georgian manifested in
1631 had given place to a hardening, as the following decisions
show.

Father Sigismund-of-St-Nicholas, an Augustinian friar
from Piedmont, who set out for China in 1730 and died at
Peking in 1767, was an advocate of building churches there
in Chinese styles and using Chinese music in their services. In

a letter in 1753 he tells how a wealthy Chinese had given him some musical instruments, and how with their help he had taught eight Chinese boys to sing the Mass chants in their own language and music, which they had done many times. In 1755 the special committee of *Propaganda* for Chinese affairs reproved Father Sigismund for this, strictly forbade the practice, and even prohibited the saying of prayers and the singing of hymns, carols or anthems in Chinese while Mass was being celebrated. Four years later it was explained to him that the prayers that must not be said in Chinese during Mass were those which the celebrant, deacon, choir or server said in Latin: were these prayers recited as they occurred by the people in their own tongue, they would appear to be part of the Mass. In 1772 the vicar apostolic of Szechwan reported that the missionaries of earlier days had translated *Veni Creator*, the *Kyrie*, *Gloria in excelsis*, the Creed, the *Sanctus* and *Agnus Dei* into Chinese, and that the people sang them thus during Mass. In reply, the Congregation said that this could be allowed, but only on condition that these prayers were said privately in a low voice, not aloud and in chorus.[25]

It is interesting to notice that what was forbidden for China in 1759 and 1773 has been a practice from time immemorial in certain German dioceses, Trier, for instance; and this in spite of the prohibition, repeated by the Congregation of Rites in 1894, of mixing vernacular singing with the liturgical texts at sung Mass.[26]

Pope Leo XIII and Montenegro

Canon Martimort remarks that 'In 1886 the concordat with Montenegro provided for a restricted use of modernized Staroslav, or *Gradjanka*, in the diocese of Antivari.' But this is a misunderstanding.

At that time Montenegro was an independent state, and its ruler, Prince Nicholas, entered into a very liberal concordat with the Holy See. The Montenegrins, Serbs in origin and speech, mostly belonged to the Orthodox Church, but there was a minority of some six thousand Catholics, most of whom were from Albania and Dalmatia, under the jurisdiction of the archbishop of Antivari. Among them, Mass was celebrated exclusively in Latin, and there was no question of introducing the Glagolitic books. But by article 11 of the concordat, the prayer for the sovereign, *Domine, salvum fac Principem* ..., was to be sung in Slavonic. But what Slavonic? Staroslav, or Serbian? Nothing is said about this, and I know of no evidence on the point. I believe, however, that it was Serbian, for newspapers writing about it remarked that the prayer was set out in the characters which the Serbs call *gradjanka*, a word that signifies 'civil', in contrast to *kirillitsa*, the characters used in Slavonic church books of the Byzantine rite.

The matter was therefore one of little or no significance for our purpose; but at the time it received considerable notice in the Catholic press of Europe as a token of Pope Leo XIII's liberality.[27]

The Living Tongue in Polish Offices

Poland has not been wholly untouched by the current whereby the Slav peoples have come to have a certain measure of their spoken languages in divine worship. The Poles have very little indeed of the 'liturgical spirit': no other people has so many popular hymns, and so many peculiarities—some of them positively grotesque—in the celebration of the Church's offices. Not only was the rosary sung during the last three days of Holy Week, but the Blessed Sacrament was exposed in a monstrance on an altar of repose, among flowers and plants and—crowning contribution of the eighteenth century—cages of little birds! I am told that such things are still done in some places; and there are plenty of other strange observances that surprise the foreigner.

But I have before me an official collection called *Cantionale ecclesiasticum*, printed at Kempten in Germany in 1878. The litany of the Saints, and the litanies of the Name of Jesus and of our Lady, the only litanies (with the more recent one of the Sacred Heart) found in the Roman Breviary, are all in Polish, including the verse, response and prayer of that of our Lady.

In Polish, too, are a number of *Supplicationes*, occasional prayers
for times of drought, floods, high winds, famine, pestilence,
war, with one of a more general kind, and a procession for All
Souls' day. There is of course always the well-worn distinction
between liturgical worship and that extra-liturgical worship
in which the vernacular may always be used; but this book
includes matter which is strictly liturgical. We have to accept
the evidence, and recognize that in some respects the Poles are
behind neither the other Slavs of Roman rite nor the Germans
in this matter.[28]

The Prohibitions of Pope Alexander VII
and Pope St Pius X

There are on the other hand certain decisions, one of them
quite recent, which seem radically to weaken the principle of
introducing a living language into the public worship of the
Western church. In 1661 Pope Alexander VII condemned a
translation of the Missal, even for private reading by the laity.
The translation was put on the Index of Forbidden Books, and
there it remained till the time of Leo XIII, when it was expunged
from the edition of 1897. As Canon Martimort points out,
Alexander VII was only following in the footsteps of the
faculty of theology of Paris in 1655, and of the convocation
of the French clergy in 1660. Who knows, he asks, whether
it was not this last decision that called forth the pope's
confirmation?[29]

The Missal alone does not contain the whole of liturgical
worship; the Divine Office also forms part of it. How, then,
can we explain the number of books in Latin and French, containing considerable parts of the office according to the
Breviaries of Paris or of Rome, that were published in France
during the seventeenth and eighteenth centuries? I have myself
come across them. For whom were these books provided if
not for the laity, who were present in greater numbers than
today at Vespers as well as Mass, and even were to be seen at
Matins? Canon Martimort is right when he says that: 'Up to

the Revolution of 1789, the clergy and people of France were at one with the Holy See in most strictly excluding any intrusion of the vernacular into the liturgy. Latin seemed to them the touchstone of orthodoxy; the spoken tongue was a symbol of recognition of the Reformers'.

Alexander VII's prohibition has now lapsed. In the middle of the nineteenth century the influence of the famous Abbot Prosper Guéranger, who restored the Roman liturgy in France, led people to substitute for total prohibition an appeal to the so-called 'discipline of the secret': the *canon* of the Mass should not be translated, because in early times it was forbidden to unveil the heart of the Christian mysteries. Nowadays this theory has everywhere been given up; and it is claimed that there never was a 'discipline of the secret'. But Dom Guéranger did not translate the canon even in his *Liturgical Year*; he simply paraphrased it.

In 1929 another Benedictine, Dom Emmanuel Caronti, published a Missal for the use of the laity in Latin and Italian, which by 1954 had reached its seventh edition. In this the whole of the canon was translated except for the words of consecration. This exception can be explained as a tactful scruple in a country where the liturgical movement is still quite in its beginnings, and only in the northern area at that; till recently hardly anybody in Italy would have thought of advocating any introduction of the Italian language into the liturgy. On the other hand in France and Belgium Missals of a similar kind were published in which everything was translated including the words of consecration. Dom Gaspar Lefebvre's *Missel-Vespéral* was approved in 1920 by Mgr Alexis Charost, who was then bishop of Lille and later on became archbishop of Rennes and cardinal. Soon after, the Flemish Missal and Vespers book published by the Benedictines of Affligem was approved by four cardinals: Mercier of Malines; Van Rossum, who was prefect of *Propaganda*; Van Roey of Malines, and Laurenti, afterwards prefect of the Congregation of Rites.[30] Alexander VII's prohibition is a dead letter today.

Nevertheless there remains a pronouncement which at first sight appears to revive these condemnations of the past. It occurs in Pope St. Pius X's *motu proprio* on sacred music (1903), and runs thus: 'The language proper to the Roman Church is Latin. Accordingly, it is forbidden to sing anything whatever in the vernacular during solemn liturgical services, and even more to sing the variable or common parts of the Mass in the vernacular.'[31]

The aim of this *motu proprio* was to put an end to a number of abuses and to restore the dignity of divine worship, which was almost wholly lost in some places, notably in Italy (The document was drawn up in Italian); and it was concerned only with music. Once the relevant parts have been sung in Latin, it by no means forbids the vernacular reading in an audible and intelligible voice of the text that has just been sung. This is done in several countries outside Italy, and it is only an application to the sung parts of the Mass of what the Spanish lady Etheria reported from Jerusalem in the fourth century, already described in the fourth section of the first chapter of this book.

It must be remembered that Italy is a very traditionalist land, and the people there are more used to Latin than they are elsewhere—which does not mean that they understand it. In the catechism that he issued in 1905, even in the first part meant for small children, Pius X gives certain common but strictly liturgical prayers in both languages: for example, *Salve Regina* and the *Confiteor*. The *Angelus*, not strictly liturgical, is given partly in Italian and partly in Latin; the psalm *De profundis* is given in Latin alone. In all Roman churches, apart from the great basilicas, a service now takes place every evening, called the *funzione*: it consists of five decades of the rosary *in Latin*, and short Benediction. The prayers after low Mass prescribed by Leo XIII are said in Latin, and the people respond in that tongue, though they certainly do not understand it. It need hardly be said that grammar and sometimes vocabulary do not emerge scatheless from these various repetitions, but the fact is there.

Bilingual Rituals*

We have now reached contemporary times, when there are numerous manifestations of the wish to see living languages given an extended use in the Western liturgy, and when Rome has given formal approbation to certain measures in that direction.

The book called the Roman Ritual did not exist before 1614, there was no *editio typica* before 1925, and it was not made obligatory for other churches of Western rite; because of these things and the very nature of its rites, it has always admitted adaptation to local usage, including small elements of vernacular speech as a secondary language. We have already seen in Chapter One of this second part that the use of this Ritual entirely in Croat and related tongues began to become general from so long ago as the middle of the seventeenth century.

After the publication of the *editio typica* of the Roman Ritual in 1925 some tendency towards introducing the spoken tongue was noticeable in successive local versions of it. For instance, in 1929 the bishops of Bavaria were given permission for what was regarded as a considerable amount of German, and this was carried further in Austria, where the Congregation of Rites approved the *Collectio Rituum archidioecesis Viennensis* in 1935. This book seems to have been deliberately designed as an essay in 'more vernacular'.

At the request of the French episcopate the Congregation of Rites in 1947 approved for use in France a Ritual (*Rituel latin-français*, Tours, 1948) which provides for a limited use of French in the ministration of the sacraments of baptism, anointing of the sick and marriage. Among the parts that must be retained in Latin are the 'form' of the sacraments, the exorcisms and the words accompanying the anointings. It may be noted that none of the psalms are translated either. It is true that the text used is that of the old Psalter, which contains not a few passages that are unintelligible without

---

* In view of further developments since this book was originally written, this section has been partly re-written by the translator.

explanation; but even the new Psalter of 1945 is far from always being crystal clear: read, for example, some of the verses of Psalm 41, used in the baptism of adults. To understand some parts of the psalms requires an initiation into the biblical way of writing and the poetical turns of speech proper to Hebrew; and not everybody can have this, even now when Bible-reading is much more common among Catholics in some countries than it used to be. From an Easterner's point of view, more could well have been translated, such as certain prayers and the exorcisms themselves; it is largely a matter of education and appreciation. In any case, the French Ritual was a great innovation, and the Church is never in a hurry in these matters.

Three years later, in 1950, an analogous book was authorized for Germany: *Collectio Rituum I* (Regensburg, 1951), 'approved by the Holy See as a supplement to the Roman Ritual. . . .' In that country, special grants existed for some time previously, and far more vernacular was now provided for than in the French book. Some of the rites, too, are revised in varying degrees, notably by the provision of a single unified rite of the last sacraments for the sick: the anointing (with a gospel, Matt. 8: 5–10, 13), viaticum, and the apostolic blessing, in that order. Here only the sacramental words must be in Latin, and for some parts the alternative Latin text is not even given, *e.g.*, for the gospel and a new prayer in litany form for the sick person. In general, all may be in German except exorcisms, anointings and sacramental 'forms'. An improved rite, including the *Magnificat*, is given for the blessing of a woman (and her child) after childbirth, and also a wholly new one for 'churching' when the child is already dead: both of these are entirely in German.

In a circular letter sent out in 1949, the internuncio apostolic to India at New Delhi recalled that eight years previously the Congregation for the Spreading of the Faith had given instructions to the then delegate apostolic to India and the East Indies for the translation of certain parts of the Roman Ritual into the languages of his territory. In 1948 Pope Pius XII had ordered that commissions be set up in each delegation apostolic to prepare such translations. The measure then was not new, and it was general in character. The general instructions were that the literary form of a language should be chosen, and care should be taken to avoid phraseology and words that were either too colloquial or too archaic. This last point excluded Sanskrit in India, of which one might at first think in view of its prestige as a sacred tongue in that country. Theological expressions were to be taken from catechisms already in use. Sacramental 'forms', exorcisms and words at anointing were to be kept in Latin; all the rest could be translated. The Austrian Ritual was suggested as a pattern.

An approved book for India was published at Indore in 1950: *Rituale parvum ad usum dioecesium hindicae linguae*. It bears the names of six bishops, those of Agra, Ajmer, Allahabad Lucknow, Patna and Ranchi, and of four prefects apostolic, of Gorakhpur, Indore, Jhansi and Jubbulpore; these are regions where Hindi is spoken, the tongue most widespread in the republic of India and officially the national language. It is written in the Devanagari script. Unlike the French book, the new Psalter is used and the psalms and much more translated. The contents, too, are more extensive. They include a rite for the reconciliation of a heretic or schismatic, the rite for the visiting and communion of the sick, the blessings of a sick child and of an adult, the recommendation of a departing soul (wholly in Hindi), thirteen blessings and a number of common prayers. On the other hand, the book omits the rite of adult baptism, which is rather surprising for a missionary country.

Other missionary territories envisaged by Pius XII's instructions are Pakistan, Burma, Ceylon, Malaya, Indo-China, Indonesia, New Guinea, China, Japan and parts of Africa, and a number of these are now provided with their own Rituals. The vernacular versions are made by a commission presided over by the papal representative in the region, and are to be used for ten years before being sent to Rome for final approval. Older Christian countries that feel the need of this reform and have taken practical steps towards meeting it are Belgium, the Netherlands, Switzerland and Portugal.

At the meeting of the bishops of the United States of America at Washington, D.C., in 1951, the Episcopal Committee of the Confraternity of Christian Doctrine was directed to study the desirability of requesting the Holy See to allow the optional use of English in certain rites, particularly those of baptism, marriage, the last sacraments and funerals. In due course the Committee, with the help of its Liturgical Committee and consultants, produced a Latin-English Ritual for submission to the American bishops, and a revised edition of it was authorized for use by the Congregation of Rites on 3 June 1954.

The principal contents of this book (*Collectio Rituum . . . pro dioecesibus Statuum foederatorum Americae septentrionalis*, Milwaukee, 1954) are the rites for the baptism of children; for confirmation ministered by a priest; for viaticum and communion of the sick, the last anointing and blessing, and for these rites in their unified form as in the German Ritual, together with the commendation of and prayers for the dying; for marriage, in various circumstances; twenty-six blessings, including the two for the churching of women from the German Ritual; and for funerals. In an appendix there is a blessing for wedding anniversaries, and a supplement gives the chant for funerals fitted to the English words.

At the baptism of children, all may be in English except the forms of exorcism, anointing and blessing, and the actual words of baptism; at the last anointing, all except the prayer at the laying-on of hands, the words at the anointings, and the prayers that follow; at the apostolic blessing at death, all except the actual absolution and blessing; at marriage, everything except the words 'Ego conjungo vos . . .'[32] and the blessing of the ring(s); at funerals, only Latin may be used for the prayers and absolutions, but other prayers etc. may be added in English at the discretion of the ordinaries. Confirmation by a priest must be wholly in Latin; the commendation of and prayers for the dying, and the blessing of the sick, of a woman after childbirth, at a wedding anniversary, and certain other blessings, may be wholly in English.

It was estimated that by the end of 1955 this new book was in use in practically every diocese of the United States. Earlier in that year the Congregation of Rites granted the use of the United States Ritual and the French Ritual, as required, to all the dioceses of Canada, and, at the unanimous request of the bishops, the use of the American book was extended to Australia.

*   *   *

I have now reached the end of this second part and may sum up.

After the first two or three centuries during which the Roman church prayed in Greek, Latin reigned alone as the one language of civilization in the West until the fourteenth century. Pope John VIII made an exception in favour of Slavonic, of which the ecclesiastical use has been perpetuated under various forms down to our own day. During the fourteenth century, the Roman liturgy or its Dominican variant were translated, wholly or in part, into Uigur Turkish, Greek and Armenian. This was approved, or tolerated, at Rome and it seems to have been the same for Albanian.

In the sixteenth century the doctrinal errors of Protestantism led to a strong reaction at the Council of Trent. But the Council nevertheless did not formally condemn the principle of the use of living languages in public worship, considered in itself: what it did do was to forbid such use on the ground that it was inopportune at that time, and because of the very great prestige which Latin still enjoyed. However, the circumstances of this prohibition were not properly understood, and it brought about a state of mind in which an opportune measure of suitability was interpreted as a formal condemnation; and this mentality governed all that was done during the succeeding centuries.

Today, the increasing desire of many clergy and people for 'more vernacular', the development of the liturgical movement, pastoral requirements and the need to make public

H

worship more intelligible if Christianity is to continue to hold people in contemporary conditions, have led to experiments some of which are not happy; and this increases the desire and need for a reform.

The Holy See is fully cognizant of the situation, and has made a number of concessions in respect of the Ritual, in missionary countries and elsewhere. That is where we are at the moment: it is a beginning, and a beginning that is susceptible of further developments.

3

LATIN INTO DEAD LANGUAGES

CHAPTER ONE

LATIN INTO SYRIAC IN MALABAR

T HERE are two special instances of the translation of Latin liturgical texts, about which I have hitherto said nothing. These are a matter of turning one dead language, Latin, into other dead languages, namely, Syriac and Ge'ez. The history of the Syriac version is not very well known, and that of the Ge'ez version hardly at all. Both are interesting and at times tragic stories, and as they touch directly on my subject it seems desirable to go into them in some detail, in which I am helped by unpublished sources of information and some personal experience. Both cases were due to lack of proper understanding and to the difficulty experienced in correcting liturgical texts that were supposed to be full of heresy; they occasioned long controversies and were eventually abandoned entirely. I take the case of Syriac in Malabar first.[1]

The Portuguese established themselves on the west coast of India during the sixteenth century, with their centre at Goa. The people of the country were heathen or Moslem, but in the south, around the tenth parallel, in the region of Malabar, was a population that had been Christian from time immemorial. Their tradition was and is (they solemnly observed its nineteen hundredth anniversary in 1952) that they owe their religion to St Thomas the Apostle who, they say, came to their country in the year 52 and suffered martyrdom at Mylapore, now a suburb of Madras on the opposite coast.

This tradition is in great part based on the apocryphal *Acta Thomae*, a document with an heretical gnostic colouring and full of fables; it was probably written by a Syrian Greek in Mesopotamia, perhaps about the year 200. That, however, is not all, and the attitude of scholars, formerly purely negative, now tends to find a certain measure of truth in the tradition; but how much it is very difficult to say. In any case, Christians are found in India at a very early date, and perhaps some were refugees from the great persecution by King Shapur II in Persia in the fourth century. About the middle of the fifth century these Christians definitively depended on the see of Seleucia-Ctesiphon in Mesopotamia, which had become Nestorian after the Council of Ephesus in 431. From this era on we clearly see Malabar depending ecclesiastically on the Nestorian katholikos living in the Sassanian empire of Persia, receiving its bishops from him, and worshipping in Syriac according to the East Syrian or Chaldean rite. No doubt the Christians in India were reinforced after the complete conquest of Persia by the Moslem Arabs in 652.

Very little indeed is known about the history of the Malabar Christians until the arrival of the Portuguese at the beginning of the sixteenth century, and the deliberate destruction of Syriac manuscripts, referred to below, is largely the cause of it. Relations between Malabarese and Portuguese were good at first, and three Mesopotamian bishops were invited to celebrate the Mysteries in the chapel that the explorers had set up. It was not till some time later that the Portuguese clergy, who knew nothing about the previous history of the local Christians, began to suspect their orthodoxy and to view their liturgy with suspicion. Their number at this time was estimated at thirty thousand families, which means at least a hundred and fifty thousand persons, living in a score of towns and numerous villages, with a metropolitan and three bishops. St Francis Xavier met the last survivor of these at the Franciscan friary at Cochin in 1549, and describes him to the king of Portugal as a good and virtuous old man. At the same time this bishop, Mar² Jacob, had already found it necessary to lend himself to a number of compromises; although he was no fanatical Nestorian and understood little about that heresy, he was virtually a prisoner at Cochin. Xavier visited the more important Syrian centres and showed himself very well disposed towards the Syro-Indians, Christians of St Thomas, as they were (and are) called.

The Latin bishopric of Goa was established in 1539 and made metropolitan twenty years later. It was just at this time, in 1551, that the katholikos[3] of the Nestorians in Mesopotamia, Mar Sulaqa, went to Rome to seek papal confirmation of his election against a rival, and obtained it; he was murdered, it is said at the instigation of his opponents, a few years later. His successor, Abd-Iso, sent two bishops to India; but the guardian of the Franciscans at Bassein thought it would be a good work to delay them there for eighteen months. He sent them on their way only after he had explained that they had no business in India, because the Portuguese archbishop at Goa was the pastor of that country; he also induced them to learn enough Latin to enable them to celebrate in the Roman way! One of the bishops went back home in disgust; the other, Mar Joseph, went to Portugal, in order to vindicate his rights. He was kept a whole year at Lisbon, and at the sixth session of the Council of Trent the Portuguese ambassador protested against what he called the intrusion of the Chaldean patriarch into a territory dependent on his royal master. Pope Pius IV was anxious not to antagonize Portugal and sought to avoid a conflict.

Meanwhile the Malabar Christians, hearing that Mar Joseph was practically a prisoner of the Portuguese Inquisition, asked for another bishop from Mesopotamia, and the katholikos Abd-Iso sent one, Mar Abraham. Abraham was careful to avoid Goa, and quietly established himself in the inland hills, where he would be free from interference. He soon saw that Malabar needed not one bishop but several. At this juncture Mar Joseph arrived in India, having succeeded in getting letters that ensured his support by the Portuguese authorities; but he had had to resign himself to the prospect of westernizing his people, at any rate to the extent of using unleavened bread for the Eucharist and wearing Roman vestments. The faithful were divided between the two bishops. The Portuguese then arrested Mar Abraham, but he escaped and went to report to the katholikos, who sent him on to Rome. Pius IV recognized that Abd-Iso was in the right and decided to apportion the Malabarese faithful between the two bishops. The archbishop of Goa and his suffragan at Cochin were informed of this decision, and Abd-Iso acted accordingly, the town of Angamali being assigned as Abraham's residence. Whichever bishop survived would succeed to the whole jurisdiction.

While Abraham was away in Rome, Joseph in India had been again denounced to the Inquisition, both in Goa and Lisbon. He was arrested and taken first to Lisbon and then to Rome, where the Portuguese ambassador counted on getting him condemned. But the impartial Roman judges recognized Joseph's perfect orthodoxy. However, he did not survive this long moral martyrdom, for he died while still in Rome.

Mar Abraham got back to India only to be arrested again. The archbishop of Goa, George Temudo, O.P., declared that his letters of recommendation were forged, and he was kept in prison until new letters should come from Rome. However, he escaped for a second time and reached the Malabar hills, where he was warmly welcomed by his flock. The Portuguese did not penetrate far into the interior and for some years Abraham was left in peace. He tactfully avoided an invitation to attend the second provincial council of Goa, and got the Indian raja of Cochin to write to the pope, with which letter the bishop sent a renewal of his profession of faith. This was in 1577. In his reply, Gregory XIII said that, knowing nothing about the persecution of which Mar Abraham had been a victim, he could give no decision. Thereupon Abraham wrote to the pope, and also invited the Jesuits of Cochin into his diocese, giving them every freedom to exercise their ministry there. He did well, for a Nestorian adventurer now appeared, calling himself a bishop. When he was arrested and sent to Lisbon and Rome, it was found he was not even a priest, and the pope ordered him to be detained in a monastery at Lisbon. But this man had left a local priest as his vicar in India, and the Malabarese faithful were again divided. These troubles went on for ten years.

In 1585 a third provincial council was held at Goa. This time Mar Abraham attended, with the encouragement of the Jesuits and the backing of the pope, and he was not too much interfered with. But, among some very sensible decrees, the council took other measures that were less so: it decided that the Roman Missal and Breviary should be translated into Syriac, together with the essential parts of the Ritual and Pontifical. Abraham signed all that he was asked for the sake of peace, and promised in the meantime to correct the Chaldean liturgical texts; this he forgot to do or, as is much more likely, was unable to do in the many places that were criticized. And in 1590 he refused to ordain candidates for orders with the rites in the Roman Pontifical; he had every right to refuse this.

This council gave to Mar Abraham as adviser and helper a Catalan Jesuit named Francis Roz, who had studied Syriac. When he was at Angamali, efforts were made to prevent Father Roz from examining the Syriac books, but in his visits to Syrian-rite churches he soon noticed that in those churches the expression 'Mother of God' was never used, but simply 'Mother of Christ'—the 'password' of the Nestorian heresy; and that in their offices, though the people did not understand the language of them, they commemorated three great 'Greek doctors', who were really the fathers of Nestorianism: Theodore of Mopsuestia, Diodore of Tarsus and Nestorius. Henceforth, Father Roz lost all confidence in Mar Abraham, and he informed Rome. He was corroborated by another Jesuit, a Maronite from Ehden in the Lebanon, Abraham George, who knew Syriac well. Father George was able to draw attention to other errors, which he found in a letter that had been surreptitiously intercepted. Pope Clement VIII was alarmed, and he told the archbishop of Goa to make a serious inquiry. The archbishop was at this time an energetic and zealous Augustinian friar, named Alexis de Menezes. He would not remove Mar Abraham, as Father Roz wanted, but waited for his death, which happened probably in February 1597. In the following year Mgr de Menezes boldly undertook a visitation

of the Syrians, which lasted several months. Though schism
was threatening, Menezes would not dismiss Mar Abraham's
archdeacon, George 'de Christo', whom the late bishop had
appointed administrator till a new bishop should be named;
but Father Roz and the Jesuit superior of the seminary at
Vaippikkotta were made his advisers. This angered Archdeacon George, who summoned a meeting of clergy and laity
who bound themselves to maintain the Syro-Malabarese rites
and customs at all costs, and not to accept any bishop who did
not come from Mesopotamia.

These Malabar Christians were an heroic people, who had
been faithful to their religion throughout many centuries,
surrounded by heathen more numerous, more powerful and
more prosperous than themselves; but they undoubtedly
provided a breeding-ground for heresy because of their
religious affiliations with the Nestorian Church in Mesopotamia. But how much exactly did they understand about it?
Certainly not much; but the material fact was there. Nor was
Mar Abraham's conduct always free from duplicity, and this
inevitably led to distrust. The mistake made by Archbishop
Menezes and Father Roz was to give too much weight to their
own Portuguese and Spanish prejudices, to be suspicious
a priori of everything that was Eastern, and to have seen no
remedy for the situation but radical suppression. This was the
mentality of all Portuguese clergy and religious, without
exception: a quarter of a century later it would cause their
expulsion from Ethiopia in similar circumstances.

*   *   *

A detailed account[4] is extant of Menezes' visitation of the
St Thomas Christians, which did not fail to raise fresh difficulties. First there was the question of the sacrament of confirmation, which was given by the priest in association with
baptism, as in all the Eastern churches; and then there was the
solemn memorial of the Katholikos of Babylon, as he was then
called, as 'universal shepherd of the Church of Christ', which
meant simply the old church of the Sassanian empire. Menezes

ministered confirmation wherever he went, refused to assist at Syrian services, and excommunicated whoever named the Katholikos instead of the Pope at the offices. Pleading a brief of Gregory XIII, who had named him bishop of Palayur (though he had not been able to be consecrated), Archdeacon George forbade candidates for holy orders among his people to receive them at the archbishop's hands; Menezes retorted by ordaining thirty-eight of them priests.

At the big centre of Katutturutti, Menezes celebrated the Roman offices of Holy Week in Latin, with the help of a choir from Cochin, and then attended the Syrian offices. On Maundy Thursday he washed the feet of twelve Malabarese priests, which made a tremendous impression on the people. This impression was deepened by the veneration of the cross the next day. The archpriest of the place, who had stirred up discontent, tried to interrupt Tenebrae by an armed demonstration; but the crowd surrounded him, urging him to submit. The archpriest refused, and the people greeted his obstinacy by an enthusiastic demonstration of submission on their own account. The same sort of thing happened at other important places, including Diamper (Udayamperur). At the same time Menezes was treating with Archdeacon George, to whom he gave a written statement of the conditions upon which he would recognize the archdeacon and confirm him in his charge. There was nothing unreasonable in these conditions, and no question of a change of rite. But Menezes was ignorant of the fact that the katholikos in Mesopotamia was in communion with Rome, and he tried to make George anathematize him. That was too much; but George accepted all the rest, only asking that he should not be required to make a public act of submission.

A synod had already been decided on in principle, and it was convened at Diamper on the third Sunday after Pentecost in 1599. At the sixth session the matter of the liturgy came up for consideration, and Archbishop Menezes revived the project, already suggested by himself and Father Roz, of translating the Roman Breviary into Syriac. The Portuguese had the idea that all the East Syrian offices in Malabar so pullulated with heresy that it was beyond the wit of man to correct them. The idea was completely false; it seems to have arisen from the exclusive use of the expression 'Mother of Christ' and from the occurrence of a few names of people who were heretical or at least unknown in the West. The Malabarese clergy, who had flocked to the synod in large numbers, strongly opposed the suggested substitution, and eventually it was agreed that their own Syrian offices should be corrected. The Syriac Bible, the famous Peshitta or 'plain' version, was incomplete in some respects, and it was decided that Father Roz should bring it into line with the Latin Vulgate. At that era they could not have done better.

Many other matters of doctrine and discipline were discussed, and some excellent decrees enacted. The Malabarese agreed to accept no bishop who had not been appointed by the Holy See, and they acknowledged all the oecumenical councils, with special emphasis on Ephesus, which had condemned Nestorianism, and Trent, which had come to an end not long before. They also accepted the jurisdiction and supervision of the Goan Inquisition. A more complete submission could not be asked, especially as the Malabarese clergy, very simple and unlearned men, had no means of knowing what it was all about. Except for a few points, they were quite in the dark. The decrees were read only in Portuguese, which they did not understand; and these decrees were drawn up in advance, and were not put before them for discussion.

The question of books of all kinds was among those examined. It was arranged that liturgical works should be submitted to the Jesuits at Vaippikkotta, to Father Roz, or to the archbishop himself for correction. There was a good number of Syriac manuscripts in Malabar, and those that were alleged to be dangerous were sentenced to destruction *en bloc*. The names of many of them are known, and some of them must be recognized as perfectly inoffensive or such as could easily be put right today: the Persian Vincentian, Father Paul Bedjan, who was of Chaldean origin, did it very well towards the end of last century. But in the sixteenth it would have been too hard a task, as the Portuguese realized, and so they cut the knot in disastrous fashion: all non-liturgical Syriac manuscripts they could lay hands on were burnt. Everybody nowadays would agree that such an *auto da fé* of what would be valuable texts was a crime, reminiscent of the legendary burning of the Alexandrian library by the khalif Omar in the seventh century.

The acts of the Synod of Diamper were signed by 153 clergy and 660 lay people. Before they dispersed, Archbishop Menezes presented to each priest an altar-stone consecrated by himself, a container for holy oils, a surplice, and other equipment of public worship. This included a Syriac translation of the principal parts of the Goan Ritual, which differs but little from the Roman. Latinization had begun in Malabar; it was to go on in more radical fashion.

Pope Clement VIII knew nothing about all these details: otherwise, the pope who had concluded the Ruthenian union of 1595 would have intervened and advised less hurry. The encouraging brief that he addressed to Menezes on 1 April 1599, took a good twelve months to reach Goa, which was then the normal time for the journey. The archbishop certainly interpreted this brief as an approval of what he was doing, and indeed his work deserved praise on more than one count; but on others it was open to the strong criticisms that have not failed to be levelled at it in later times. The Synod of Diamper was simply a diocesan synod, and as such it was not necessary to submit its acts to Rome for examination. A written account of it was sent to Clement VIII, but death prevented him from seeing it. His successor, Leo XI, was pope for less than a month, and the report, finely bound and bearing Clement's arms, eventually came to rest in the archives of the Society of Jesus, where the present writer has seen it. The acts of the synod were printed in Portuguese at Coïmbra in 1606, but it was soon forgotten; the Congregation for the Spreading of the Faith, which was not established till 1622, appears to have known nothing about the synod till Raulin published his

Latin edition of its acts in Rome in 1745. After that, the Congregation several times directed that its prescriptions be observed, for want of better ones. But long before that the imprudent or tactless measures of Menezes and some of his successors had taken effect and been the cause of evils which have begun to be remedied only in our own day.

Many priests, secular and regular, followed the Portuguese into India, of whom the Jesuits kept in most constant touch with the Malabarese. It was, then, to be expected that Archbishop Menezes, determined to allow no Mesopotamian bishop in the country, should think of appointing someone of Latin rite, and preferably a Jesuit, to the see of Angamali, making it suffragan to Goa. No other solution was possible, for the Syrian rite was suspect, there was no Malabarese priest well enough qualified, and in virtue of the *padroado*[5] no one but a Portuguese could be appointed. The obvious candidate for the office was Father Francis Roz, and he was in fact preconized at the consistory of 20 December 1599, the more willingly in that Rome was always nervous lest there be an outbreak of Nestorianism in India. But there was a difficulty about the new bishop's place of residence, and it was desired to placate the Malabarese, who were not anxious to depend too closely on Goa, that is, on the Portuguese; and so Pope Paul V dismembered the diocese of Cochin and made Angamali an archbishopric with its seat at Cranganore. It was thus independent of Goa, but had to send representatives to its provincial councils.

*   *   *

Despite inevitable clashes, the Portuguese prelates of Angamali-Cranganore, all Jesuits, governed the Malabarese without too much difficulty until 1652. In order to maintain a unified spirit and to avoid the disturbing variety of policy and conduct that had come about in other places, the Jesuits allowed only clergy of their own Society to work in Malabar. An Italian Dominican, relying on his office of missionary apostolic, disregarded this in 1628, when he opened a school for clerics in which he taught Syriac; he was practised in the language and the Jesuits tended to neglect it. This was enough to please the Malabarese clerics, who knew little Syriac or none at all, but nevertheless regarded it as a national inheritance. The archbishops at Cranganore still had to go on putting up with the presence beside them of a Malabarese archdeacon, who really had all the influence; and George, still archdeacon at this time, knowing he could never attain the episcopate himself, petitioned Lisbon that the Dominican in question might be named as their future bishop. But this was impossible too, as he was an Italian and not a Portuguese.

In 1646 another Dominican, but Portuguese, who was bishop of Cochin, complained to Rome about the Jesuits' exclusiveness, and discontent was aggravated six years later when a Syrian monk, probably an adventurer, turned up at Mylapore declaring he had been sent by the pope to be patriarch of Malabar. He managed to get in touch with the Malabarese archdeacon, now Thomas Parambil ('de Campo'). But the monk was promptly seized by the Portuguese and taken to Goa, where (as some said) he was tried by the Inquisition and sentenced to the stake in accordance with the ways of the time. It was given out that he had been accidentally drowned, but nobody believed it. The Malabarese had wanted to examine this man's credentials for themselves, and on 3 January 1653 a big meeting was held in front of the church at Mattancherry; this assembly took a solemn oath no longer to recognize the archbishop at Cranganore and to drive the Jesuits out. A few months later, Thomas Parambil produced a letter alleged to have been written by the Syrian monk, which purported to authorize the Malabarese to choose a bishop of their nationality; as there was nobody to consecrate him, Archdeacon Thomas had himself 'made bishop' by twelve priests.

It was at this time that war broke out between Portugal and Holland, commercial rivals in India, which soon ended in almost complete victory for the Dutch, who were Calvinists by religion and very bitter against the Catholic Church.

Thomas Parambil thought to profit from this and, without troubling about the inconsistency of his proceedings, he addressed himself to the Jacobite (monophysite) patriarch of Antioch, who lived at Mardin in Mesopotamia: from him he asked that a bishop should be sent to Malabar who would confer true episcopal orders on himself. This took place in 1665.[6] Now, Nestorianism denies that the Blessed Virgin Mary is Mother of God, but it acknowledges two natures in Christ, the divine and the human; while Monophysism is the opposite error, acknowledging Christ's divine nature alone. These distinctions did not trouble Thomas Parambil, nor were they made by the simple Malabarese; what they wanted was a bishop from among their own people, and they followed their schismatic and heretical leader in large numbers. This was the origin of the Jacobite or monophysite community in Malabar which, with certain derived bodies, continues to this day.[7]

Those among the Malabarese who held aloof from this separatist movement—at first not more than four hundred families—asked the Barefooted ('discalced') Carmelites, with whom they were in good relations, to look after their interests in Rome. The Congregation for the Spreading of the Faith was opposed in principle to a monopoly of any nationality or religious order in Malabar, but it could not disregard the *padroado* privilege without precipitating a conflict with the Portuguese government. The Congregation therefore devised the system of vicars apostolic, which has since been applied in all mission territories where a regular hierarchy of bishops is not yet constituted: a vicar apostolic is a titular bishop who governs a delimited territory in the name and under the direct authority of the Congregation, by delegation from the Supreme Pontiff. Immediately the news of Thomas Parambil's revolt had reached Rome, an Italian Carmelite, Joseph Sebastiani, had been sent to Malabar as visitor apostolic. He succeeded in winning over the Malabarese minority element called 'Southists', who live in the southern part of the country and claim to be descended from ancestors who were, they say, converted to Christ by St Thomas the Apostle himself. After

Sebastiani had reported to Rome, he was consecrated bishop in private and sent back to India. The exclusiveness of the Portuguese had been modified in face of the threat from the Dutch, and they welcomed the Italian papal visitor; he took advantage of this to be active among the Malabarese, with such success that he weaned large numbers from the schismatic movement and greatly strengthened those who had remained faithful. Before he was forced out of the country by the Dutch in 1663 he revealed his episcopal character and, in virtue of the wide powers he had received, consecrated as bishop the most suitable man among the Malabarese clergy. This was Palliveetil, or Parambil, Shandy (Alexander de Campo), cousin of Archdeacon Thomas Parambil.[8]

The Congregation for the Spreading of the Faith, always afraid of possible Nestorianism, would have liked the Malabarese to have themselves asked to be aggregated to the Latin rite; but it neither would nor could force them to this step, which would have caused a definitive schism and would have been contrary to the fundamental principle of the Congregation touching respect for Eastern rites. In the event, it twice tried giving the Malabarese a vicar apostolic who was at least Indian, if not of Syrian rite; but these designations were not happy, both because the men chosen were unsuitable and because of the Congregation's anxiety to protect the rights of the archbishop of Cranganore and the bishop of Cochin, provided these prelates would satisfy their obligation of residence, from which they used to dispense themselves too easily. The problem became insoluble: there were three disagreeing parties among the Catholic Malabarese, and the Dutch would allow neither the archbishop of Goa to intervene nor clergy from Europe to exercise their ministry. At one moment Pope Innocent XII (1691–1700) thought he could ease matters by getting the Emperor Leopold I of Austria, then ruler of the southern Low Countries, to allow religious toleration to the Calvinists there in exchange for Dutch permission to allow Belgian, German or Italian priests to work in Malabar.

I

At length a Carmelite was made vicar apostolic of the Malabarese in 1701, and he was accepted by all the Catholics; but other difficulties arose, due to Portuguese obstinacy and to the appointment of Jesuits to the sees of Cranganore and Cochin, whom the Malabarese did not want. Moreover, the Verapoly seminary, the nursery of the Malabar clergy, had to be closed soon after 1682 for lack of funds, and was not opened again for over eighty years. There was no longer any hope of a bishop being chosen from among the Malabarese priests, for they were unable to offer properly qualified candidates. The few clergy of various foreign nationalities were at odds among themselves, and anyway were difficult to recruit. Things were made worse when in 1782 an Indian priest of Latin rite, Dr Joseph Kariattil, being in Lisbon, was nominated archbishop of Cranganore by Queen Maria of Portugal. Here were the Latin-rite Catholics getting an Indian bishop, while the Syro-Indians continued to be under their Carmelite vicars apostolic from Europe. And when Archbishop Kariattil was taken ill and died immediately after getting back to India in 1786, the Malabarese said he had been made away with by the Europeans. Henceforward the Catholic Syro-Indians too had but one thought: to get an Indian bishop, and if possible one of themselves. But there was no hope of that when they even had no regular seminary; Verapoly was reopened in 1764, but as yet it could hardly be regarded as such.

*   *   *

It was one of the Carmelite vicars apostolic, a Pole named Nicholas Szostak, who brought about the first printing of a Syro-Malabarese Missal, during the later part of the eighteenth century. The Synod of Diamper had suppressed two of the three forms of eucharistic Liturgy used in Malabar (as they are still used by the Catholic Chaldeans in Iraq), the reason given being that they bore the names of Nestorius and Theodore of Mopsuestia. It has long been admitted on all hands that these attributions are fictitious. From early in the seventeenth century their own ecclesiastical calendar had been replaced by

that of Goa, practically the same as the Roman, and the
liturgical epistles and gospels had been rearranged to accord
with those in the Roman Missal. Only the one form of
eucharistic Liturgy remained East Syrian, and even that was
tampered with: the altar bread was unleavened, the chalice
was withheld from the laity, ceremonies were imported
from the Western rite and its vestments imposed, while the
Malabarese clergy had to dress like those from Portugal.

This would have been the moment to begin a real reform,
by giving the Malabarese the Chaldean Missal which was
published in Rome for the first time in 1767. This, indeed,
was what the majority of the cardinals of *Propaganda* wanted;
but the faithful in Malabar had now got used to the mutilated
Diamper liturgy, and the Chaldean Missal contained an Arabic
translation of the scriptural lessons that would have been no
use in India. So the Missal was printed from a manuscript
sent from Malabar; it first appeared in 1774 and has been
republished several times. It is wholly in Syriac.

The British régime in India was far more liberal than the
Dutch, and in 1831 it was possible to form a congregation of
the Carmelite third order regular of the Syro-Malabar rite.
It took definitive form in 1855, under the vicar apostolic
Bernardino Baccinelli, O.C.D., who also worked hard for the
formation of a good pastoral clergy, getting rid of the in-
efficient private clerical schools and centralizing all sacerdotal
training at Verapoly. His successor, Leonard Mellano, O.C.D.,
in 1876 published a sort of ferial office, arranged more or less
according to East Syrian tradition, with a supplement for
certain feasts, of which some parts are translations from the
Latin. In the same way the offices of Holy Week and certain
special observances, such as the blessing of ashes and of palms,
are partly in accordance with Eastern tradition and partly
borrowings from the Roman rite, translated into Syriac. The
Goan Ritual is likewise translated, except for funerals, which
still keep their Syrian forms, with some Western interpola-
tions. All is in Syriac, with no admixture of the vernacular,
Malayalam; so the people understand nothing of what they

say or sing in church, except, of course, for 'popular devotions'.[9]

Long accustomed to the alteration and virtual ruin of their liturgy, the Malabarese were never really reconciled to being under the jurisdiction of European prelates. Any ecclesiastical adventurer who turned up amongst them, expressing sentiments of loyalty to Rome, was sure to be given some degree of credit. In 1787 the administrator of Cranganore was one Thomas Pareamakel, a Malabarese of Latin rite, and the Malabarese petitioned both Rome and the queen of Portugal to have this man as their bishop. When this failed, they turned to the katholikos of the Catholic Chaldeans, Joseph IV, but he had retired to Rome, and their appeal was delivered to his *locum tenens*, John Hormizd, the metropolitan of Mosul. Hormizd ordained a bishop and dispatched him to Malabar; his good faith in so doing was so patent that Rome did not take a severe line with him, and eventually itself told a Chaldean bishop, of Salmas in Persia, to go and try to clear up the situation in India. The visit never in fact came off, it is not clear why; but people remembered these things. The Congregation for the Spreading of the Faith, however, was unwilling to invoke the help of bishops of a church, the Chaldean, that was itself experiencing grave troubles at that time, and because of the manifest impossibility of their being able successfully to govern a people so different from themselves in race (the Malabarese had been completely Indian for long ages), language, social conditions and now even in liturgical rite.

Not much later, in 1838, there began what is often called the Goanese Schism, a movement of some of the *padroado* clergy against the institution of vicars apostolic in general, and particularly against the recent attribution to the vicar apostolic of Malabar of territory where Christianity was rapidly increasing, territory which they alleged belonged by right to the sees of Cranganore and Cochin, and so to the Portuguese *padroado*. Some Malabarese priests became involved, and in 1849 they appealed to the katholikos of the Chaldeans, Joseph

VI Audo, to send them a bishop from among his clergy in Mesopotamia; the request was repeated in 1852, this time accompanied by a threat to 'turn Jacobite' in case of refusal, and Audo sent it on to Rome.

There was some substance in their complaints: that many of the Malabarese were left without religious instruction, that some of their clergy were insufficiently zealous, that the Carmelite missioners were too few and not always up to their work, that there were more than four hundred thousand faithful without a bishop of their own rite, while the far fewer Latin-rite Catholics had three vicars apostolic in the region. But the Chaldean katholikos was not the man who could remedy this situation. Joseph Audo was badly informed and he was very opinionated; time after time he returned to the charge, with his argument from his early predecessors' historic rights over Malabar, which no one denied. It was difficult to come to terms with a man of that stamp, even if the parties would have been satisfied by a purely formal agreement, such as a nominal dependence of the Syro-Malabarese on the Chaldean hierarch. Eventually, Audo defied Rome's express prohibition of interfering in the affairs of Malabar; he ordained and dispatched a bishop, Thomas Rokkos, a totally incapable man, who nevertheless at once gained many followers. Rokkos was soon recalled, but in 1874 Audo sent another bishop, Elias Mellus, and a schism broke out afresh; it lasted till Audo's submission in 1877. But there is still a small irreconcilable group at Trichur, the Nestorian 'Mellusians', left over from these troubles.

*   *   *

Pope Leo XIII brought all these dissensions to an end when in 1886 he concluded a concordat with Portugal, whereby the extent of the Lisbon *padroado* was delimited and the Goanese Schism thus healed. Returning to a scheme that had already been mooted in Rome after Mar Joseph Audo's submission, and had previously given good results when not thwarted by unfavourable circumstances, the pope in the same year appointed two vicars apostolic, Latins for the moment, for the Malabarese alone; these prelates were assisted by vicars general of Syrian rite, who had the privilege of *pontificalia*. Ten years later the two vicars apostolic were replaced by three, who were Malabarese of their own rite (a fourth, for the 'Southists', was appointed in 1911). They received episcopal consecration at the hands of the delegate apostolic in India, Archbishop Ladislaus Zaleski, and naturally according to the Western rite, since there was no Catholic Eastern bishop in the country.

A question that at once presented itself was: What Pontifical would these new Malabar bishops use? There was a manuscript one in Syriac, that had belonged to Bishop Palliveetil Shandy and was kept as a relic; but no one thought of this at the moment, and when it was looked at later it was found to be in a very bad state and useless. The bishops had a choice of the Chaldean Pontifical, that of the West Syrians (both only in manuscript and unknown in Malabar) and the Latin one of Rome. It was natural enough in the circumstances that they should consider only the third, and that Mgr Zaleski, who was a Pole, should agree with them. Later on, in a report to *Propaganda* in 1909, he expressed the opinion that Rome was mistaken in looking on the Malabar rite as a derivative from the Chaldean, and that in reality it was closer to the Western rite than to those of the East. It must be admitted that external appearances were a justification for this view; but he was equally wrong when he went on to say that 'Hitherto there has been too much sacrifice of the Catholic spirit of the Eastern churches to the purity of their rites': in other words, that to be a good Catholic one must be as 'Latin' as possible. Anyway, he asked in 1896 that the Roman Pontifical should be translated into Syriac for the Malabar bishops, seeing that the use of this language would counter the objection that rites were being mixed. Meanwhile, ordinations and other episcopal ministrations would be carried out in Latin.

The Congregation for the Spreading of the Faith, very poorly informed and having at its disposal no one really competent in such matters, had agreed to this request, and asked the Malabar bishops to proceed with the translation. Years passed. In 1905 Mgr Zaleski returned to the charge, alleging the old misleading reasons: the Malabar rite was only a modified Roman rite, or better, that the Synod of Diamper had created a new rite which, approved or at any rate tolerated by the Holy See for three hundred years, had now the right to be considered as an authentic liturgy of the Catholic Church. The translation of the Pontifical had been begun but was not yet finished, and meanwhile some of the Malabarese clergy were agitating that Malabar should be once more attached to the Chaldean katholikate. In view of what had happened under Joseph Audo, this agitation was full of danger.

In an address presented to Pope St Pius X on the occasion of his episcopal jubilee in 1908, the Malabarese bishops expressed their desire for the approbation of the Syriac version of the Pontifical, and *Propaganda* urged them to hurry on the text. Another ten years passed, and it was still not forthcoming. In 1918 the new delegate apostolic in India, Archbishop Peter Fumasoni-Biondi, again drew the Congregation's attention to the inconvenience and inappropriateness of using two liturgical languages in the course of one ceremony—it would have been more exact to say two quite different rites in one ceremony; and eighteen months later the Malabarese vicars apostolic repeated his observations in a joint letter.

At the end of 1923, Pope Pius XI set up a hierarchy in ordinary for the Malabarese, with a metropolitan see at Ernakulam and three suffragan bishoprics. One of its first acts was to call for the Syriac version of the Pontifical. After once again refusing the use of the Chaldean one, as being strange to them, they were at long last able to send the translation to Rome—after thirty-five years of delay and shilly-shallying.   ★   ★   ★

The Eastern Congregation, which was now in being since 1917, entrusted the examination of the translation to the Chaldean bishop of Amadiyyah, Mar Francis Daud; he adversely criticized some of the grammar, literary style and terminology, and finally rejected it. The whole thing would have to be done again; but nobody was found equal to the task in Malabar. In 1932 the archbishop of Ernakulam, Mar Augustine Kandathil, raised the question again; a really good translator could certainly be found in Rome or in Syria or in Iraq. But the Congregation was hesitating: there had already been far too much hybridization of the Malabar liturgy, and this projected Pontifical would make it much worse. Their opinions were asked from a congregational consultant, a Carmelite who had long ministered in Malabar, and the delegate apostolic in India: all three were in favour of a Syriac translation of the Roman book. But when the learned producer of the *Patrologia orientalis*, Mgr René Graffin, was asked if he would be willing to print the translation once it was brought to a successful conclusion, he replied firmly that he would never do it, even if ordered to by a superior: for, he said, to allow this translation would in his judgement be a bad thing, and to agree to print it would be to co-operate in a mischief.

Mgr Graffin made this categorical statement by word of mouth in January 1933. He was a man known everywhere for his competence in all that touched the Christian East, for his knowledge of Syriac, and for the esteem in which he had been held by four successive popes, and especially by Pius XI: and his clear opinion increased the general state of uncertainty. The secretary of the Eastern Congregation, Cardinal Sincero, was not the man to make up his mind lightly; everybody knew his sympathy for all things Eastern, and during the thirty-five years this affair had dragged on there had been considerable development of ideas.

In my essay called *L'Uniatisme*, which attracted considerable notice in the circles concerned after its appearance in 1927, I said of the latinization of the Malabar liturgy: 'A reaction is difficult; nevertheless we need not yet wholly despair of one.'[10] Cardinal Sincero had read this booklet carefully, and he asked me what I thought. I replied in November 1933 in a *votum* of sixty pages. I began by showing that the Malabarese are of Chaldean or East Syrian rite, and I sketched the vicissitudes which it underwent among them. I passed their liturgical books in review and described their state. The provision asked for seemed to me impossible, for liturgical and canonical reasons. I pointed out that the Synod of Diamper, which was no more than a diocesan synod, had never been approved by the Holy See, and never would have been. I emphasized that India was in a state of evolution, and that the Malabarese would sooner or later realize that their liturgy in its present state was a monstrosity, from which Protestantism did not fail to profit and which was a scandal to the local Jacobites, a stumbling-block in the way of their reconciliation with the Catholic Church. In my opinion, the reaction had to start in Rome: no other way was possible; and the best course would be to leave things as they were in Malabar for the present, and to concentrate at once on the revision of the Chaldean Pontifical.

Two other consultants were called in: the late Dom Placid de Meester, Benedictine, professor of liturgy in the Greek College at Rome, and Mgr Eugène Tisserant, then pro-prefect of the Vatican Library. Both agreed with me.

The matter was discussed at the full session of the Eastern Congregation on 19 November 1934. The cardinals were naturally divided, some being in favour of the provision that had been asked for by so many bishops and delegates apostolic, others advocating the use of the traditional Chaldean Pontifical. In his audience a fortnight later Pope Pius XI decided the matter in his usual authoritative and forthright way: 'Latinization is not to be encouraged among the Easterners. The Holy See does not want to latinize but to catholicize. And then, half-measures are ungenerous and they do not bring good results. So continue *in statu quo*, but organize at once a commission for the revision of the earlier Pontifical, which can be printed part by part.' The pope named three people whom he expected to find figuring on this commission, and later approved two other members, together with two Chaldean priests to advise on technical points.

The commission began its work in the spring of 1936 and

continued for three years. Cardinal Tisserant had now succeeded the deceased Cardinal Sincero as secretary of the Eastern Congregation, and the commission was presided over by Father James Vosté, O.P., who had lived many years among the Chaldeans in Iraq and knew Syriac well. From the Chaldean katholikos, Mar Emmanuel Thomas, there was obtained an exact copy of the Pontifical he used, and also an ancient manuscript of one from Mosul, while photographic copies were made of other manuscripts in several Europe libraries. The Pontifical was restored on the basis of these, and a Latin version was then made, which was subjected to careful theological and liturgical examination. There were remarkably few adjustments of doctrinal significance to be made: simply some turns of phrase to be altered and names of heretics of the Nestorian era to be expunged. The whole was approved in a full session of the Congregation on 3 July 1939, and its decision was confirmed by the pope six days later. The book now had only to be printed.

Here there were unexpected set-backs due to delay in receiving two responses from the Holy Office (which were not given till 25 March 1942), to the death of Father Vosté in 1949, and to the failure to find a printer properly equipped for the work, whether in Europe, Iraq or Malabar. The well-known house of Wilhelm Drugulin at Leipzig had the necessary type and had printed Father Paul Bedjan's books, but it was now in the Soviet zone of Germany and not available. But happily it was found that the press of St Joseph's University at Beirut could undertake the work, and the Chaldean Pontifical, for the use of both the Chaldeans and the Malabarese, is being produced there at the present time (1954).

But not only that. The Eastern Congregation has set up a commission to prepare a new edition of all the Malabar service books, and its work also is going ahead. Some of the clergy and more educated laity in Malabar are showing signs of a desire for a purification of their rite; some, too, would like Malayalam to be introduced into their public worship, even if only to a limited extent, in place of the Syriac that none of the laity understand and which the clergy themselves know only more or less. The bishops will do as the Apostolic See decides.   *   *   *

Two more Malabarese dioceses have recently been established, of Palai (1950) and Tellicherry (1954); this last is conterminous with the Latin diocese of Calicut, where there are three times more Syrians than Latins. Over the past sixty years or so the diocesan clergy has been altogether renewed by the priests trained at the pontifical seminary at Puthenpally, transferred in 1932 to Alwaye. Here Malabarese students form the majority, and the Sunday Liturgy is celebrated alternately according to the Syro-Malabar and the Roman rites. Unfortunately, Syriac is but little taught and the pertinent rite not much studied: the seminary is conducted by Carmelites of the Biscayan province, who are therefore mostly of Basque origin. The congregation of Malabarese Carmelite tertiary fathers and brothers is in a highly flourishing state, and nine or ten congregations of women have been established. The population is very prolific, and the Catholic Malabarese now number well over a million; aspirants to the priesthood and the religious life are so numerous that the bishops normally ordain only those who have a patrimonial title: the others are to be found all over India, having by force of circumstances to enter seminaries and religious orders of the Western rite.

Since the disasters that have overtaken the Ukrainians of Galicia and the Rumanians of Transylvania, the Malabarese form the largest Catholic community of any Eastern rite; and it is their rite that has been mistreated more than any other—but improvement has at last begun and will be maintained. Though there was a slight movement in that direction at the beginning of the present century, all idea of their depending on the Chaldean katholikos in Iraq has now been abandoned. Encouraged by national patriotism, the Malabarese call themselves Indians, as in fact they are and have been for many centuries, and every year the conversion of numbers of non-Christians strengthens the Catholic element.

In the translating of parts of the Latin liturgy into Syriac for the use of the Malabarese, Rome itself had no part, if we except the supplement to their Ritual for the baptism of adults: it was all done under private initiative. When they came to be known there, these translations were accepted as they stood; but eventually Rome refused to allow the process to go on so that such hybridization should not be made worse. This means that, at any rate on this point, the work of Archbishop Menezes and the Synod of Diamper has been rejected.

CHAPTER TWO

LATIN INTO GE'EZ IN ETHIOPIA

IN the second case of turning Latin into another dead
language things did not happen in altogether the same way,
but the final upshot was exactly the same, and for the same
reasons. This time it was a matter of Ge'ez, once the spoken
tongue and now the sacred language of Ethiopia.[1]

Early in the sixteenth century the Christian, but at least
materially heretical, king of Ethiopia, the *negus* Lebna Danghel,
sought the help of the Portuguese against Moslem aggression,
and a military expedition was maintained from Lisbon from
1520 to 1527. The chaplain to this expedition brought back a
letter from the *negus* in which he expressed his submission to
Pope Clement VII. In 1541 the Moslems again attacked, and
King John III of Portugal again sent help. The medical officer
with this second expedition (as with the first) was one John
Bermudez, who gave it out in Ethiopia that Pope Paul III had
appointed him patriarch there, though he was no more than a
priest (as well as a physician), even if that. The whole thing
was made up by interested persons, but it received some
credit in Ethiopia, where there was already a desire to be
free from ecclesiastical allegiance to the Coptic patriarch of
Alexandria.

Thereupon a religious mission to Ethiopia was decided on
and entrusted to the Society of Jesus, being accepted by St
Ignatius Loyola himself. He had his doubts about Bermudez;
and on making inquiries found that the man had been discovered to be a fraud but that, to avoid an open scandal, the
head of the mission was to be instructed to watch whether he
behaved himself and discharged his duties satisfactorily. If he
did, he was to be conditionally ordained and confirmed in

office, privately; if not, he was to be deposed and the leader of
the mission, Father John Nuñez Barreto, was to take his place.
Accordingly, Nuñez Barreto was nominated 'patriarch of
Ethiopia' and, together with two other Jesuits who had also
been consecrated bishops, set out for Africa in 1557 by way
of Goa. Directly Bermudez got wind of this he left Ethiopia
and went back to Portugal, coolly declaring that he had lost
his bulls of appointment during the disaster that had overtaken
the second Portuguese expedition. He was believed, and
nobody thought of checking his statements in Rome, where
St Ignatius had kept the secret. Bermudez was given a pension
by the king and he retired to a hermitage near Lisbon, where
he lived quietly till his death in 1570. Before he died he
published, with the approval of the chief inquisitor of Portugal,
an account of the 1541 expedition which was really the auto-
biography of himself. It was not till this work was reprinted
in 1855 that the whole story was made public.[2]

Nuñez Barreto never got to Ethiopia, dying at Goa in 1561,
but his companion, Andrew d'Oviedo, had reached his
destination four years before. The then *negus*, Galadewos
(Claudius), was at first well disposed towards the Catholic
Church, but he soon changed his mind and inaugurated a
period of difficulties that lasted till 1563. But from then until
his death in 1577 Bishop d'Oviedo was able to work in peace.
No reinforcements were sent to the mission from Rome or
Lisbon, because the Portuguese king did not believe it was
serving any good purpose. However, after the last of Barreto's
companions had died, he was replaced in 1603 by Father Peter
Paez, S.J. and several others. These were at once more successful, and eventually in 1614 the *negus* Susneyos (Sisinnius)
became a Catholic privately, making his action public eight
years later. He abolished monophysism, the observance of the
Sabbath (Saturday), and polygamy, putting down strong
opposition with an energy no less strong, and using armed
force in the process. Father Paez died in 1622 and, at the
request of Susneyos, the Holy See nominated Alfonso Mendez,
S.J., in his place, with the title of patriarch of Ethiopia.

The year after Mendez arrived in the country, 1626, union of the Ethiopian Church with Rome was solemnly proclaimed. A score of Jesuits, with as many Ethiopian auxiliaries, traversed the land, verifying the validity of baptisms and ordinations, and imposing the observance of the Gregorian calendar and the fasts and abstinences of the Roman discipline and all this not without military aid. What is more, Mendez wanted to impose the use of the Roman liturgy translated into Ge'ez, in all ignorance repeating the mistake that was made in Malabar. These excessive measures called forth protests, underground resistance and finally open rebellion: the word went round that Susneyos and the Jesuits were plotting to hand Ethiopia over to the Portuguese. Mendez had to yield on matters he ought never to have interfered with: abstinence on Wednesday instead of Saturday, the old calendar, the traditional liturgy. This encouraged the opposition to further efforts, and in 1632 Susneyos was forced to grant religious toleration. He died in the same year, and at once his son Fasiladas (Basilides) banished Mendez and his clergy. They returned to Goa in 1636.

Ethiopia remained closed to the Catholic Church for two hundred years. In 1788 an Ethiopian priest, George Gabra-Egziabeher, was ordained bishop at Rome by a bishop of Byzantine rite, by express order of Pope Pius VI, and departed to his homeland, accompanied by a Franciscan friar. He was murdered soon after his arrival.[3] But in 1837 the two Irish-French explorers, Antony and Arnaud d'Abbadie d'Arrast, going on a scientific expedition into Upper Ethiopia, took with them to Cairo as their instructor in Arabic an Italian Vincentian named Joseph Sapeto, who had learned the language in Syria. Father Sapeto managed to instal himself at Adua, in order that he might study Ge'ez and the various spoken dialects of the country, as well as its history and monuments. He did not call attention to himself by doing a lot of apostolic work, but his sojourn had been authorized by the Congregation for the Spreading of the Faith, and in 1839 it was decided to set up a prefecture apostolic for Abyssinia,

Upper Ethiopia and the neighbouring regions, with no
definite boundaries to the west and south. This decision was
largely due to a long report that Antony d'Abbadie presented
in Rome, setting out reasons why Catholic activity was called
for in Ethiopia. Father Sapeto became the first prefect, but
learning—and even politics—was more in his line than active
apostleship, and he was released from his duties in 1842. He
was succeeded by another Italian Vincentian, from Naples,
Justin de Jacobis; he laboured in the country for twenty-two
years and died there in 1860, having been consecrated bishop
as first vicar apostolic of Abyssinia a dozen years previously.[4]

*   *   *

The difficulties in the way of apostolic work in Ethiopia have
always been many and various. The Ethiopians are a very
intelligent people, and very proud of their civilization: a
civilization which, though it is now developing rapidly, may
appear primitive to Westerners, but is none the less much
higher than that of African peoples who have lived in complete
isolation from the rest of the world till recent times. Ethiopian
Christianity, early infected with heresy, has acquired various
usages due to Jewish influence on the one hand and heathenism
on the other; such as the practice of circumcision, the
observance of the Sabbath, numberless superstitions, a long-
established polygamy, at least among the ruling class, and
slavery, though of a special kind that was less oppressive than
the slavery which made such ravages elsewhere in Africa.

Printing was not known in the country till the end of the
nineteenth century: books were, and still often are, copied by
hand, and their necessary material, parchment, is more
difficult to obtain and more expensive than paper, or even the
papyrus of ancient Egypt. Ethiopian manuscripts often
contain the most diverse matters, all mixed up together. The
liturgy of worship has been affected accordingly. Fundamentally it is the old Alexandrian rite of the Copts of Egypt,
but with Syrian and many local elements, the latter even now
sometimes improvised during the course of a service. The

liturgical books are not properly and logically arranged; the contents of the Ritual, for example, are scattered here and there in manuscripts containing other things: the rite of baptism, say, may be found written after an historical chronicle and preceding a collection of magical formulas or medical pre-scriptions. An examination of Ethiopian manuscripts in European libraries soon makes this clear.

To such difficulties as these was added the lack of preparation among European missioners. They could not be blamed. In the sixteenth century the monk Tasfa Seyôn succeeded in casting the requisite type in Rome and printed the New Testament and some liturgical fragments, and in the seven-teenth century a German, Job Ludolf, really initiated Ethiopic studies; but these studies remained in their infancy until the second half of the nineteenth century. The Capuchin Franciscans and the Vincentians (Lazarists) are devoted more directly to apostolic work than to learned research, though of course this too is an instrument of apostleship. The Society of Jesus already had a tradition of learning by the seventeenth century, but the Jesuits engaged in Ethiopia were Portuguese, with an inveterate conviction that everything eastern is bad, or at least highly suspect of heresy; they showed this in Malabar, and it is easy to understand that Mendez thought of replacing the Ethiopic rite by the Roman liturgy in Ge'ez.

In 1846 Rome detached part of the prefecture apostolic of Abyssinia to form the vicariate apostolic of the Gallas, a warlike people who live around Gondar, Amhara and Shoa. The first vicar was a Capuchin from Piedmont, William Massaia, who laboured in Upper Ethiopia for thirty-five years. He then returned to Italy, where he charmed Leo XIII by his accounts of his experiences: so much so that the pope made him a cardinal in 1884 and paid for the printing of his memoirs, *Trenta anni in Abissinia*. At the very beginning, writing about Egypt where we went first, Massaia gives his impression of Eastern clergy and their rites of worship. It is most unfavourable.

At the end of his life his views had not changed. In a report

K

he sent to the Congregation for the Spreading of the Faith in 1882, he denied that the Ethiopians had any such thing as a true liturgical rite. He looked on it as an aggregate of a number of usages that had been

> arbitrarily introduced, and were provisionally tolerated by the Church to avoid worse evils. . . . Liturgical unity is more to be desired than variety. . . . National pride, the begetter and guardian of all these different rites, which are an obstacle and a very great difficulty in the way of apostleship in the unfortunate East, is equally the unhappy origin of the misshapen Ethiopic rite. . . . Variety of rites . . . is not a beauty but, today anyway, a hindrance in the Church.[5] She accepts them as a lesser evil, lest a poor people be lost. . . . The prohibitions of passing to the Latin rite and of conferring orders according to that rite are unnecessary measures. It would be much better to leave everything to the prudent discretion of the vicars apostolic.

Further on in the report Mgr Massaia quotes a passage from his memoirs in which he relates how, not being able to find his way among the fourteen forms of anaphora (canon) in the eucharistic Liturgy of the Ethiopians, he fell back on having the Latin Mass translated into Ge'ez, with the rubrics in Amharic. He had a few Ethiopian priests of their own rite, and he says these priests were surprised by the simplicity and doctrinal precision of this Mass, and that they asked to be allowed to celebrate it privately within the sanctuary, which among the Ethiopians is nearly always wholly enclosed; the choir meanwhile would sing this and that outside. In the end Massaia agreed to this, with the reservation that they would have to conform to further instructions from Rome should such be given. After considering the report, the Congregation decided that nothing should be altered for the moment.

Ten years later, in 1892, the vicar apostolic of Abyssinia, Marcel Touvier, a Vincentian, expressed the same opinions:

> The [Ethiopic] Mass hardly displays the character of sacrifice or oblation. . . . Mr d'Abbadie assures me that he has never come across a single manuscript that formed a complete Ritual,

and he does not believe such a thing exists. . . . May I not be
allowed to conclude that it is desirable and morally necessary
to give up this so-called Ethiopian Ritual and to impose the
Roman Ritual translated into Ge'ez? . . . With this [Ethiopic]
rite, it is impossible to form souls in the ways of piety, to produce saints, we shall never have sincere and solid Catholics; for
everything in this rite draws people away from the Roman
Church, from religion and from God. . . . Will not the time
come when it should be considered whether, in order to restore
this Ethiopian nation to Catholicity, it would not be better and
even necessary to give it the Roman rite, purely and simply?
In my humble opinion there is no other way of making all these
Christian communities of the East sincerely Catholic. . . .

Justin de Jacobis saw more clearly. He had been given the
faculty—and it is the first instance of it—to adapt himself to the
Ethiopic rite and to celebrate according to it; but in the end he
never used this faculty, because of the then impossibility of
finding texts that were dogmatically and liturgically reliable.[6]
He had not been given any preliminary preparation for his
work, for there was no one qualified to give it at that time.
However, he courageously set himself to learn the languages
and to consult relevant manuscripts, which the dissident
clergy and monks were not very willing to put at his
disposal. At the most he was able to revise the common
parts of the eucharistic Liturgy, and doubtless one anaphora;
he was not able to do anything positive with the Ritual,
its different parts being scattered about manuscripts whose
texts were far from being always in agreement with one
another.

It may be remarked that it was just the same with the
Byzantine rite before its books began to be printed in the
sixteenth century: the manuscripts displayed a mass of variant
readings, sometimes of importance, and offices were found
completely differing for the same day. But is so happened that
the Orthodox Greek books were all published in the same
place, at Venice, and the printer-publishers soon got into the
habit of copying from one another. In the seventeenth century

the patriarch of Moscow, Nikon, revised all the Russian books in accordance with Greek exemplars from Venice (incidentally occasioning thereby the great schism of the Starovery), thus bringing unity to the Slavonic books and, through the Slavs, those of the Rumanians. A single type was thus established. It was also the same in the Western church before Gutenberg; but after the coming of printing Rome soon took charge, so that today, apart from the Ambrosian rite of Milan and those of certain religious orders, a uniform Roman rite is followed practically everywhere. Things were not working out like that in Ethiopia.

In face of the liturgical anarchy there, Justin de Jacobis had to fall back on translating from Latin. His Ritual, copied and recopied by hand, was used by some Ethiopian priests, while others gave it up in favour of the Latin original. One can understand the conclusion at which Mgr Touvier arrived in 1892: that 'it is desirable and morally necessary to give up this so-called Ethiopian Ritual and to impose the Roman Ritual translated into Ge'ez, at any rate for the sacraments other than baptism. But even for baptism, which includes confirmation, I am still disposed to advocate the gradual substitution of the Roman rite. . . .'

The position was much the same as regards the eucharistic Liturgy. As for holy communion, the Ethiopic rite requires that it shall be given under both kinds. And so it always was in Eritrea[7] until the coming of the Italian Capuchins in 1895; they imposed celebration with unleavened bread instead of leavened bread, and communion in one kind only, except in solemn Masses and on certain occasions. Such were the rules laid down by the vicar apostolic Camillo Carrara in his *Rules for Priestly Life drawn up from the new Canon Law*, which was printed at Asmara in the Tigré dialect in 1920; and they were more or less observed. In the rest of the country, under the jurisdiction of the French Vincentians, things took a very similar course. Mgr James Crouzet, vicar apostolic from 1888 to 1896, even forbade priests to give confirmation immediately after baptism (which is the normal practice of all Eastern

churches), on the ground that they had not got any chrism.
But he had only to give it to them!

*   *   *

It was then that the controversy began between the holders
of two opposed opinions: there were those who advocated
that the Ethiopic-Alexandrian liturgy should be put in order,
with corrections where necessary for doctrinal reasons, and
then brought into full use; while others wanted it to be suppressed altogether and a Ge'ez version of the Roman books
put in its place. This disagreement lasted for over forty years,
from 1895 to 1936.

On 4 February 1895 the Congregation for the Spreading of
the Faith had to consider various questions respecting Ethiopia,
including liturgical ones. On this subject it had no material to
go on except the reports from Mgr Massaia and Mgr Touvier
that have been quoted above, and it is not surprising that these
reports strongly influenced the decision taken. The full session
comprised seven cardinals, of whom Miecislaus Ledochowski,
Luigi Galimberti and Vincent Vannutelli were well known
for their sympathies for the East; of the views of the others I
know nothing. The rescript was as follows: 'That the most
holy Father be asked that the Roman liturgy in the Ge'ez
language may be given to the Ethiopians of Abyssinia, and
also that [the vicar apostolic] may decide if there be a general
and lawfully prescribed custom of a faculty for the priests of
that country to confer the sacrament of confirmation after
baptism.' The *mens*, however, that is, the explanation of the
resolution, much used in full sessions, is very guarded. It ran:

The missioners are warned that they must use every care and
much prudence in carrying out this change, as well as in getting
rid of everything abnormal in the actual way that baptism is
conferred. Moreover, they must be careful not to make a
translation of the Latin liturgy into the said language [Ge'ez]
without the previous authorization of the *Propaganda* Congregation. The prefect apostolic of Eritrea is to be asked to take

measures for the making of a translation with the help of priests native of the country, and in due course this translation shall be sent to the Congregation with a view to its proper revision.

Five days later Leo XIII approved these decisions. One might be surprised at this pope doing so, only a few weeks after the publication of his famous constitution 'Orientalium dignitas', whose very object was to stop latinization, and at a time when the pontifical commission for the reunion of the East was in full action. Had the matter been publicized, would it not have been regarded as a striking demonstration of Rome's duplicity? But in fact there were only four possible courses open, which were admirably set out by Cardinal Parocchi, the rapporteur of the full session. They were (1) to impose the Latin rite pure and simple; or (2) to translate its books into Ge'ez or Amharic; or (3) to revise the existing rite, supplying missing parts, such as ordination and pontifical services, from another Eastern rite; or (4) to leave things as they were, a mixture of Ethiopian and Western usages. It certainly looks as if there was a gross illusion going about at the time, namely, that to have the Roman liturgy in Ge'ez would not prevent the Ethiopians from being part of the Eastern church and of Eastern rite.[8] As if the 'Glagolites' of Dalmatia were prevented from being part of the Western church because they use the Roman Missal in Slavonic!

Meanwhile, two important events had recently taken place. First, with the encouragement of Mgr Crouzet, the Vincentian J. B. Coulbeaux, the most competent in local things of the Western clergy in Ethiopia, had revised seven of the fourteen eucharistic anaphoras, and a limited edition of the Ethiopic Missal had then been published at Keren in 1890. With the short Ritual of Mgr de Jacobis and the Psalter with supplements published in 1893,[9] which could serve as an Office book, it seemed a good thing to stop there for the moment.

The second event that affected the development of the

ritual and linguistic problem was one of the political order
that had ecclesiastical consequences. The priest Joseph Sapeto,
who has been mentioned above, had given up all ecclesiastical
activity and devoted himself wholly to secular affairs; and in
1869 he bought the bay of Assab on behalf of the Florio-
Rubattino shipping company: in 1882 this property was ceded
to the Italian government. This was the beginning of the
Italian colony of Eritrea, which now forms part of the empire
of Ethiopia. The statesman Crispi wanted, and then demanded,
that, in exchange for the *exequatur* granted to Mgr Sarto (later
Pope Pius X) for the civil regularizing of his position in the see
of Venice, the Holy See should replace the Western clergy in
Eritrea by others who were not French, and put a bishop at
their head. This is what lay behind the decree of *Propaganda* of
13 September 1894, whereby a provisional prefecture apostolic
was established for Eritrea and entrusted to the Capuchin
Franciscans of the Roman province. The Vincentians then
withdrew to Ethiopia proper.

The newcomers were completely inexperienced, for there
was no organization to give them the required training—the
Oriental Institute was not yet born. So far as rite and language
were concerned they found themselves in almost the same
position as Justin de Jacobis half a century before, with the
difference that there were now some good Ethiopian priests,
with a liturgical practice that was imperfect but sufficiently
promising.

In these circumstances it can be appreciated how Rome
preferred the fourth of Cardinal Parocchi's suggested lines of
action: things were to be left as they were for the present.
And the more so because the first prefect apostolic, Father
Michael of Carbonara, had hardly arrived in Eritrea when he
saw what a grave obstacle to Christian reunion a change of
rite would be, even a change that conserved the Ge'ez language.
Nothing more was done till 1903, when the prefect of *Propaganda*, Cardinal Gotti, consulted the heads of mission on the
subject, Father Edward Gruson, for Ethiopia, and Father
Michael, for Eritrea. It appears that the last-named replied only

in vague terms, if he replied at all.[10] Father Gruson in turn consulted the leading clergy, and they all spoke unhesitatingly in favour of the maintenance of the *status quo*. Father Gruson simply reported this response, adding a request that the short Roman Ritual in Ge'ez should be printed. Again nothing more happened for several years.

Then in 1907 the Congregation for the Spreading of the Faith made further inquiries. Father Michael of Carbonara replied promptly. He set out clearly the difficulties of substituting the Roman rite, even in Ge'ez, for the Ethiopic: the Missal would have to be translated first and that alone was a heavy task, though not impossible. Then, what about the Ethiopic calendar, which has many peculiarities, and all the numerous Ethiopian saints? And particularly what about the church chant, to which the Ethiopians are very attached indeed? To change their rite would make a bad impression on Catholics and would drive away the dissidents altogether; whereas they gladly came to Catholic services in the Ethiopic rite, because they found them celebrated with decency and good order, especially funerals. In a word, Father Michael was opposed to changing the rite.

Rome wanted fuller information about the real state of the Ethiopic liturgy, and sent out a questionnaire a few months later. It can be deduced from the replies of the heads of mission that, among the dissidents, the Ethiopic liturgy, while complete and adequate in theory, was disfigured by many abuses and insufficiencies in practice. Services were extremely long (but the Ethiopians like them long). Some of the fourteen anaphoras had been composed by heretics. The eucharistic wine was not wine but the juice of dried grapes steeped in water. Baptism was often invalid through alteration of the form, or because it was not uttered at the moment of immersion. There was no episcopally hallowed chrism, but only ordinary oil blessed by a priest simply by a sign of the cross. Confession was made more or less as it should be only occasionally; generally it was more like a parody. The sick were rarely anointed, because the clergy clung to the letter of the rubric, which requires the assistance of seven priests. Ordinations were doubtful, for one never knew whether the only bishop, a Copt from Egypt, observed his rite exactly, and often he did not observe it at all. The wedding service was inordinately long, and people believed that marriage was indissoluble only if the parties had received communion together. Funerals also were very long, with nine absolutions. Except for monks, the Divine Office was not obligatory (but that is in accordance with the true Eastern discipline).

It should be noticed that some among the reported divergences are only matters of discipline: for instance, blessing the water for each baptism, instead of once a year, the blessing of the oil of catechumens by a priest, instead of by a bishop, the absence of salt from holy water.

In view of these replies, Rome decided that the short Ritual of Justin de Jacobis should be printed, after it had been carefully revised by Father Coulbeaux and the senator Ignatius Guidi. The last-named was one of the most distinguished scholars in things Ethiopian of his day, and personally he was opposed to this translated book; but he agreed to do the work out of politeness. It appeared at Rome in 1910, very well printed, with a simple *imprimatur* from the prefect of *Propaganda*. It comprises only the forms for the baptism of children, absolution, viaticum, the last anointing, the apostolic blessing *in articulo mortis*, the recommendation of a departing soul, the burial of a child, marriage and the blessing of holy water. Funerals of adults were to continue to be carried out according to the Ethiopic rite. Three years later a second edition of the Missal was published at Asmara, this time provided with the traditional fourteen anaphoras. It too had the simple *imprimatur* of the Congregation for the Spreading of the Faith.[11]

Everything seemed in order for the time being, and perhaps a good many years would have passed without these questions being reopened, had it not been for the intervention of an excellent Ethiopian priest, Abba Takla Maryam Semharay Selim; he was a man of ordinary ecclesiastical education, with no scientific training properly so called, self-taught, but he knew his rite well and loved it passionately. I knew him personally very well, and sometimes helped him in the drawing-up of his communications to the Holy See. He was one of those who contributed most to the abandonment of translations from the Latin into Ge'ez and the gradual restoration of the Ethiopic rite.

Abba Takla Maryam was born at Keren in 1871, and was educated by the Vincentians in his own country. After being ordained priest, he was sent to minister for a dozen years in the territory of the Boghos, a heathen tribe among whom there lived some dissident Christians and a minority of Catholics. In 1910 he was transferred to Jerusalem as head of the little Catholic Ethiopian hospice there, and in 1927 he was appointed spiritual director of the Ethiopian College at Rome, which was then temporarily housed at San Stefano dei Mori, behind St Peter's. Two years after its removal to the fine building that Pius XI had erected for it in the Vatican gardens, Abba Takla Maryam stayed for a time in Paris, and on his return became professor of Tigré at the University of Rome. Here he remained, writing and doing research among the Ethiopian manuscripts in the Vatican Library, till his death in 1942.[12]

While still at Jerusalem, he in 1913 sent his first report to *Propaganda*, criticizing the Ge'ez Ritual of 1910 and pointing out that the Ethiopians had a complete Ritual of their own, differing but little from that of the Copts. He also criticized the Keren Missal of 1890 from which, he said, too many things had been left out through the desire to shorten it. He returned to the same subject in the following year, complaining particularly about Father Coulbeaux's alterations and omissions in the various anaphoras. All these observations were communicated to the heads of mission in Ethiopia; they naturally defended their predecessors' work, and produced copious quotations to show that Abba Takla Maryam's criticisms were at least exaggerated. This epistolary contest perhaps had something to do with Takla Maryam's eventual

call to Rome, where the Eastern Congregation, established
ten years before, was far from being displeased to have him
handy.

Soon after his arrival there Takla Maryam launched an
attack on the practice, introduced about 1894, of using unleavened instead of leavened bread, at any rate in 'private'
celebrations of the Eucharist, to which the vicar apostolic in
Eritrea, Mgr Camillo Carrara, had now added a prohibition of
giving communion in both kinds except at solemn Liturgies.[13]
Then, too, the sanctuary-veil had been taken away in the
church at Keren; priests reconciled from the dissidents
were conditionally ordained in public, instead of in private;
and the use of the Western funeral service in Latin also
scandalized the dissidents. The Eastern Congregation consulted Abba Kidane Maryam Kassa, soon to be a bishop,
who was in Rome taking the course in law at the Gregorian
University; all the reply he could make was that these
things had now become habitual and it was better to make
no change.

In the following year, 1929, Abba Takla Maryam made
another report, this time on the Ethiopian College in Rome,
and I have had plenty of opportunities to satisfy myself that his
criticisms were justified. The buildings of the college are handsome and convenient, but its chapel is completely Western.
Every day, even Sundays, the eucharistic Liturgy was the
Latin Mass, a few days of the year only excepted. Vestments
were more and more Western, the daily prayers were all Latin.
Here as in Eritrea, Western usages were introduced into the
Ethiopic Liturgy: the gospel read at the northern end of the
altar, genuflexion at 'And was incarnate' in the Creed, and the
words 'and from the Son' added after 'who proceeds from the
Father',[14] elevations at the consecration, with genuflexions
from then till the communion, and so on. When in 1923—and
I saw this myself—a solemn service was held at the Greek
College in memory of Mgr Julius Tiberghien, a great
benefactor of the Eastern Congregation, and the last
absolutions were given by a representative of each rite in

turn, people were astonished to see the Ethiopians appear dressed in surplice and cope. . . .

*   *   *

It may be asked why the Eastern Congregation did not react sooner in face of this hybrid situation and the strong criticisms of it. The fact is that this new institution did not get properly into its stride before 1927, the year in which Cardinal Sincero became its secretary, that is, for practical purposes its prefect.[15] When Pope Pius XI appointed him, knowing his capacity for work, the cardinal hesitated to accept, pointing out that he was a jurist, who had never concerned himself about Eastern matters. 'All the better,' replied Pius, 'you will not have preconceived notions.' Cardinal Sincero tackled his work courageously, but there was so much calling for attention that the question of public worship and its books in Ethiopia had to be postponed for a time.

There was a more urgent matter to be dealt with in that country. Catholics were increasing in number, and it was time they were definitively organized. So in 1930 the Eastern Congregation established an independent ordinariate for the faithful of Ethiopic rite, and put at its head Abba Kidane Maryam Kassa, with the episcopal title of Thibaris.[16] This priest, who was already pro-vicar for the Ethiopian clergy under the vicar apostolic Mgr Celestine Cattaneo, was born at the great Catholic centre of Hebo in Eritrea in 1886 and was trained at the Latin patriarchal seminary of Jerusalem. He was certainly the man most worthy of the new office, but owing to his upbringing all his sympathies were with the 'latinizers'. When, after his episcopal consecration by Cardinal Sincero at the Ethiopian College in Rome, he made his solemn entry into Asmara, he was enthusiastically received by the people and their clergy, who were delighted that they had at last got a bishop chosen from among themselves: it was the more a pity that his habiliments on that occasion were those of a bishop of the Western rite. Afterwards he returned to Rome to take part in the work of the commission for the codification of Eastern canon law.

There now arose the question of what rite the bishop should use for ordinations. There was no Pontifical in the Ge'ez language; the Ethiopian Catholics had hitherto been subect to Latin-rite bishops and their priests had been ordained according to that rite. The sole dissident bishop was always a Copt from Egypt, and his proper Pontifical was the Arabic-Coptic book. Bishop Kidane Maryam knew neither Coptic nor Arabic, and he certainly would want to use the Roman Pontifical with the relevant parts translated into Ge'ez. In this he had the strong support of the former vice-rector of the Ethiopian College, the Capuchin Father Mauro of Leonessa, who had worked for a long time in Eritrea and was in favour of latinizing. Three months before Abba Kidane Maryam's appointment became official, Father Mauro had addressed a long memorandum to the Eastern Congregation in which he sought to prove, not very scientifically, that Ethiopian ordinations should be by means of the Latin rite. This was what had always been done; the Catholics were used to the four lesser and three major orders, instead of the four only of the East; they admired the Roman ceremony, and so did the dissidents; the ordinand would understand the prayers—such were the sort of arguments used. This memorandum was soon followed by another and similar one.

At the same time Father Mauro was pressing Bishop Kidane Maryam to hasten the translation of the relevant parts of the Roman Pontifical. They had won over the new assessor of the Eastern Congregation and Cardinal Sincero himself, both of whom were as yet inexperienced in these matters, and by the first month of 1931 the Ge'ez version was duly approved: but the cardinal wisely added *donec a Sancta Sede aliter provideatur*, 'until such time as other provision may be made by the Holy See'. The book, 256 pages quarto, was superbly printed by the Vatican Press in an edition of twenty-two copies only, and it was in use by June of the same year.

There was no lack of protests at this swift *fait accompli*. It

was no longer 1895, and knowledge of things Ethiopian was
no longer in its infancy. I had watched what was happening
and, though I had not been asked, I decided that it was my
duty to offer some observations. Accordingly, on 27 October
1930, I transmitted a long document to the assessor of the
Eastern Congregation. In it I set out the history of the
Ethiopic-Alexandrian liturgy, and described the revision of
the Arabic-Coptic Pontifical and Ritual made in the eighteenth
century by the Coptic priest (afterwards bishop), Raphael
Tuki; this was done under the auspices of the commission for
the correction of Eastern service books, and led to the magnificent edition of the Coptic books published in Rome in 1761–63.
Of this edition I gave a detailed analysis. I advocated the
translation of the ordination rites into Ge'ez, on a basis of the
literal Latin version of the Coptic text made by Scholz and
published in a collection that is well known to scholars and
theologians.[17] This translation could be done by Abba Kidane
Maryam Kassa, and revised first by the learned scholar in
Ethiopian, Sylvain Grébaut; then by the Ethiopian Vincentian,
Abba Tasfa Sellasie, whom the *negus* Haile Sellasie had
commissioned to translate the Swiss civil code into Ge'ez and
Amharic; and by Abba Takla Maryam Semharay. As the new
Ethiopian bishop did not know the Coptic pontifical rites, I
suggested the composing of a Ceremonial with the help
of the very precise descriptions given by the Dominican
Vansleb.[18]

It was love's labours lost. The assessor read my document
with careful attention, but his mind was made up: however,
perhaps I was responsible for the '*donec a Sancta Sede aliter
provideatur*'—and that was something. In any case, the whole
business made such a noise in Rome that in 1933 the Eastern
Congregation resolved to reconsider the question.

The president of the Pontifical Oriental Institute, Father
Émile Herman, S.J., categorically declared himself against the
innovation of conferring orders by the Roman rite in Ge'ez.
He warned against the bad impression it would make on
dissident Christians in Ethiopia, and refused to assimilate the

case to that of the Malabarese and their use of the Roman
Pontifical. One can only speculate what he would have said
could he have foreseen that, only the next year, Pope Pius XI
would refuse to countenance the continuation of this and
order the preparation of the Chaldean Pontifical, and that
within a dozen years the revision of the hybrid Malabar
liturgy would be in hand. The Benedictine monk Dom Placid
de Meester, so well known for his work on Byzantine liturgy
and monastic law, protested against the latinisms and other
innovations at the Ethiopian College, and Father John Hanssens,
S.J. added his voice; the latter was a professor at the Gregorian
University and the Oriental Institute who had recently shown
his deep knowledge and understanding of Eastern liturgies of
worship.[19] And then Abba Takla Maryam Semharay broke
another lance against the Karen-Asmara Missal, convicting it
of seventeen mistakes. This charge was sent to Bishop Kidane
Maryam, who did not attempt to traverse it, but only replied
that, since these were in the Missal, they must be complied
with.

At the end of 1935 the Eastern Congregation again inter-
rogated three of its consultants, with a clear question: What
must be done to restore the Ethiopian rite to its primitive
purity?

The first consultant began his reply by setting out principles.
Latinization had had its day: the attention of both Catholics and
non-Catholics was too wide awake to the matter to tolerate
it. Reform was in the air among the dissidents: for the first
time in history, the dissident Coptic patriarch of Alexandria
had in 1929 visited Ethiopia in person, and had ordained five
bishops in place of the single one previously to be found
there. The texts were in existence: they had only to be
examined from the doctrinal point of view, purged of inept
or undignified passages, and indications given of what might be
omitted at will, always, of course, keeping the spirit of the rite
in view. Modern devotions used by the Catholics ought to be
expressed in forms that accorded with their rite. He proposed
that all its texts should be printed and published; he asked that

Western clergy sent into Ethiopia should be properly prepared beforehand; he explained how a mentality hostile to the Ethiopic liturgy had come to be developed among priests who were otherwise zealous and worthy; and he emphasized that the innovations they had introduced should be abolished. This *votum* did great honour to its author, Father Émile Herman, just mentioned, of whose outstanding services to the commission for codifying Eastern canon law I was myself a witness.

The second consultant was none other than Mgr Eugène Tisserant, at that time pro-prefect of the Vatican Library. He was wonderfully qualified for his task: a graduate of the School of Eastern Languages at Paris, knowing Ge'ez, and having recently travelled in Ethiopia; being in good part author of the monumental catalogue of the 286 Ethiopian manuscripts at the Vatican; having a vast bibliographical knowledge in all the languages of European learning; knowing the various Eastern liturgies of worship in some detail, and respecting and loving them. Of all those who had been consulted before, Mgr Tisserant was the only one (except Takla Maryam Semharay) who recalled the founding of the Ethiopian monastery of St Stephen 'of the Blacks' close by St Peter's in 1774, the Office that was regularly celebrated there, Tasfa Seyôn's edition of the New Testament and of the ordinary and three anaphoras of the eucharistic Liturgy, with a Latin version of the *Ordo communis* and the rite of baptism, and that this work was not intended simply for scholars but for use in Ethiopia. Mgr Tisserant did not doubt that, had the circumstances been more favourable, Bishop Justin de Jacobis would certainly have passed to the Ethiopic rite; he pointed out that Bishop Massaia's long Ethiopian experience had been almost entirely among Moslems and heathen; and he remarked, too, that other Western priests had been in contact only with Ethiopian rural clergy, who were often illiterate, and that these Europeans had not, nor even tried to have, any relations with the great monasteries of Debra Libanos or Lake Zaway. He then gave a complete list of all editions of Ethiopic liturgical texts made in Europe and of translations into various languages, ending with a suggested programme for a future publishing commission, even adding the names of possible members of it.

The third consultant was not a specialist on the matter in hand but was highly competent in the Byzantine rite; he had spent four years in Jerusalem and been able to observe the Ethiopian monks there from close up. From a body of selected texts he showed that the Ethiopian rite is not a myth, and that it contains doctrinal formulas of unimpeachable orthodoxy, both in the eucharistic Liturgy and the ordinary of the Divine Office. He passed all the liturgical books in review, citing them according to partial translations hidden away in collections or other works where no one would think of looking for them: it gave evidence of the vast extent of the consultant's reading. His conclusion was that the Ethiopic rite must most certainly be restored, and he looked to the Ethiopian College in Rome to do it. The author of this *votum* was Father Severian Salaville, of the Augustinians of the Assumption.

The field was won; and there is no doubt that Cardinal Sincero would have at once acted accordingly, but he died suddenly on 7 February 1936. Pope Pius XI met the situation by putting at the head of the Eastern Congregation a man one of the finest of whose titles to glory (for he has many others, and merits before God too) must be his activity in promoting the revision and publication of Eastern liturgical books: Eugène Tisserant.

He was speedily created cardinal, and as soon as he was able he formed the commission which he had advocated. It was at work from the summer of 1937 to that of 1943, and consisted of four members, with the valiant Takla Maryam Semharay as assistant; he was already very ill, and could not be of much help, but he had the consolation of seeing his lifelong ideal triumph before he died. For the basic text of the Missal the commission did not take the Keren-Asmara Missals, but two reasonably good editions published by the dissidents, one at Dire Dawa (1926) in Ge'ez alone, the other at Addis Ababa

L

(also in 1926), containing also an Amharic version and explanations. That was always the mode of procedure; to take the best non-Catholic edition, correct it if necessary, and then reprint it. The new Missal was approved in a full session of the Eastern Congregation on 26 June 1944, sent at once to the Vatican Press, and published in the following year. It is a beautiful volume, a small quarto of 226 pages, two columns to a page, printed in red and black, with three fine reproductions in colour of Ethiopian eikons, a little stylized. This *Mashafa qeddâsê*, 'Book of Liturgies', comprises the ordinary of the service and, this time, seventeen anaphoras (canons); according with Eastern custom, the text of the biblical lessons is not included, but only that of the eucharistic sacrifice itself.

Meanwhile there had been procured a copy of the Ethiopian-Alexandrian Ordinal that had been drawn up from the Coptic-rite book for the use of the dissident bishops, of whom there is now one for each Ethiopian province. After a careful revision this Ordinal was printed, and published in 1940. From then on Bishop Kidane Maryam Kassa used it for ordinations, and the Ge'ez version of the Roman Pontifical was put away. But the new Ordinal does not contain the ordination of bishops: when Abba Kidane Maryam died in 1951, his two successors, one for Eritrea and one for the rest of Ethiopia, were consecrated according to the Latin rite by Cardinal Tisserant.

The Ordinal was followed by the equivalent of the Greek Horologion, the *Mashafa sa'tat*, 'Book of Hours', for the Divine Office. This appeared in 1952. Of the strictly necessary books, there now remains only the Ritual, which is at present being worked on.

In the same year it was decided that the Ethiopian students at the Capuchin seminary of Gaggiret must keep their own rite, and there was thus initiated a purely Ethiopic branch of the order of Capuchin Friars Minor. By 1954 it already had a dozen members.[20] In view of the circumstances of their work, it was judged best to follow the biritual system for the present; but all idea of translating Latin liturgical texts into Ge'ez is entirely given up. In spite of his advanced age, the rector of

the Ethiopian College in Rome set himself to study the rite
and its language in order that he might be able to celebrate
therein on suitable occasions. The hybridisms of which Takla
Maryam Semharay complained have mostly been eliminated,
and the rest will go bit by bit. Who could possibly have
foreseen this in 1895, or even much later?

CONCLUSION

THESE pages have been written with an apostolic end in view: to provide some exact documentation, complete so far as possible, for those who are seeking to obtain the introduction of a measure of living languages into the public worship of the Western church. The liturgy is the Church's true common prayer, and it is meant for everybody, not for the clergy alone. The people can take part in it to the full only if they understand it: and not everybody can afford to buy a bilingual Missal, or has the ability and education necessary for the proper use of it. Moreover, till recently a classical education enabled many cultured people to understand Latin; but classical education is now in decay, and the number of people who know Latin gets fewer every day. Quite involuntarily, the community of faithful is split between two categories: those, generally the economically better off, who have some classical culture and can understand and appreciate the Roman liturgy, and those who do not understand it properly and have no means of doing so. The Church is the society of all the faithful; but if there be, to use the modern jargon, a sort of bourgeois aristocracy among them, then the exclusive use of Latin at public worship tends not to unify but to divide.

In his address to the third International Congress of Liturgical Studies, held at Lugano in Switzerland in 1953, the archbishop of Bologna, Cardinal Lercaro, quoted these words of St Pius X, written hardly three months after he became pope: 'The first and indispensable source for the acquiring of this [true Christian] spirit is active participation in the sacred Mysteries and in the solemn public prayer of the Church.' Elsewhere in his address the cardinal said:

Pius X had hoped and recommended that the faithful unite with the clergy in the Church's prayer of Vespers on Sundays and feastdays; but since his time many have taken to the Divine Office, in whole or in part, and use it as the norm of their devotion, uniting themselves with their clergy at least in spirit. Hence the Breviary has had to be translated into modern languages to fill a widespread need. . . . The encyclical letter '*Mediator Dei*' of our present pope . . . , after expounding [certain] principles, goes on to add, for the realm of practice, its approbation and praise of the various forms of the faithful's active participation in the Mass already introduced by the liturgical movement. Moreover, opening up luminous vistas for further adaptations of the liturgy to new historical situations, the encyclical states the principle of the changeableness of the liturgy in its accidental forms, and affirms the relative usefulness of the spoken tongue therein.

After referring to the Easter vigil and other reforms of Pius XII, Cardinal Lercaro harked back to other concerns of St Pius X and concluded that 'It would seem that the widespread hope of our time, that the biblical lessons at Mass may be read by priest or ministers in the people's language, fits harmoniously into the framework of the reforms realized or desired by that holy pope'. And, with a passing allusion to 'the usage of the Eastern liturgies, which often have bilingual, and sometimes trilingual, texts', the cardinal commended the hearing of 'the word of God in [our] own mother tongue *directly and immediately from the mouth of the minister*' (emphasis mine). The second petition (*votum*) of the Congress quoted these words textually and made them its own; and the third ran:

> In order that the people may participate in public worship more easily and more beneficially, this Congress respectfully asks that the local ordinaries may be empowered to enable the people (if it be judged opportune), not only to hear God's word in their own language, but also as it were to respond to it, by praying and singing in their mother tongue, even during a Mass that is sung.[1]

*   *   *

The conceding of a larger element of vernacular speech in the liturgy would also be of the utmost value for the evangelization of non-Christians.

For the Moslems the hour of grace has not yet struck: there are only rare individual conversions, generally of persons of note, such as Father Abd al-Jalil, O.F.M., and the late Mgr Paul Mulla, who was professor of Moslem and Turkish institutions at the Oriental Institute in Rome. Arabic, the language of the Koran, is a sacred tongue for Moslems, understood and spoken, in several dialects, by many millions of people. Now, there is a Christian liturgy celebrated in Arabic, that of the Melkites, Catholic and Orthodox, in Syria, Palestine and Egypt, who use that language almost exclusively in their Byzantine rite. The Little Sisters of Jesus, working among them in the difficult Hauran region, have already adopted their rite, and their superioress at Damascus has taken Syrian nationality in order to avoid any suspicion of political interest—on which she must be congratulated. In the midst of the Sahara, at Father de Foucauld's hermitage at Tamanrasset, the superior of the Little Brothers of Jesus, Father R. Voillaume, celebrates the Mysteries in the Arabic language and the Byzantine rite. Maybe no Moslem there will be converted to Christ, but it is at any rate an example and a precedent. What a help that liturgy could have been to Cardinal Lavigerie when, before he had St Ann's Melkite seminary at Jerusalem, he founded Arabic-speaking villages in North Africa after the cholera epidemic and famine of 1867.[2]

Or again, there is in India an attractive and interesting people called Parsis, who, as their name shows, originated in Persia; they emigrated thence in face of the Moslem Arab invasion in the eighth century. They had been subjects of that Sassanian empire whose persecution of Christians drove some Syriac-speakers into India. The great Parsi centre is Bombay, and they form a veritable aristocracy, highly educated, very prosperous, and self-sufficient.[3] Their religion is that of the ancient Persians, Mazdaism or Zoroastrianism, reputedly dualistic but really a monotheism; they are commonly regarded as fire-worshippers, but in fact they reverence fire as the purest symbol of the Deity, and their morality is summed up in the axiom 'Think well, speak well, do well.' Mazdaism has some striking analogies with the Jewish revelation and even with certain Christian beliefs.[4]

Yet a Parsi never becomes a Christian, any more than they try to spread their own beliefs. They are content to remain as they are, taking pride in their descent from the Persians of old and in the ancient language, Pahlavi (sometimes wrongly called Zend), in which their sacred books are written. As things are, if one of them became a Christian he would be swallowed in the mass of Latin Catholics or of Protestants, and that a Parsi could not stomach.

But many of them know something of Christianity, and a way could be found of approaching them, through an Eastern rite. That of the Malabarese is indicated, for it was the liturgy of the Christians of Persia. When its restoration has been effected, it would only have to be translated into the language spoken by the Parsis, Gujarati, or partly into Pahlavi. Thus they would not lose their historic heritage, and would remain sufficiently differentiated, for Bombay is a long way from Malabar, and their rite would give them a special place among their immediate fellow Catholics.[5]

Japan is another possible case. Here Russian missionaries of the Orthodox communion, with the Byzantine liturgy in Japanese and a practically wholly Japanese clergy, laid the foundations of a Christian community that now numbers some fifty thousand souls.[6] A Jesuit priest of the Byzantine rite, destined for Russia but unable to go there under the Soviet régime, is now working in Japan, celebrating the liturgy in Japanese, and it may be that this approach has a future before it.

To express my opinion in a sentence—and I am not alone in holding it—the Eastern liturgy, so ceremonious and impressive, is certainly more suited to Asiatic peoples than is the Roman liturgy: the latter may be more 'practical', but its sobriety is more adapted to the mentalities and temperaments of the West. Were the Russians to be rid of communism, autocracy and Byzantine formalism, and to be reconciled with Rome, their church would recover the vitality that it lost under the tsars, when it was in bondage to the civil power and often used as an instrument of politics: and it would then be in a position to win the whole of Asia to Christ. We are most certainly a long way from that, and the Soviet system is as strong as ever. Only God knows the future; and only God can remove obstacles that are insurmountable by men, and bring the great idol with head of gold and feet of clay crashing to the ground, as in the prophet Daniel's vision. Being what I am, a priest of the Byzantine rite, I may be allowed to end by thus conjuring up what is today a dream but one day may be a reality.

NOTES

Part I

Chapter One

1. [Aramaic is a Semitic language, with close affinities to Hebrew. Syriac is another form of it.—*Trans.*]

2. [In Italy, Gaul and the Iberian peninsula, Latin 'gradually developed into Italian, French, Spanish, etc., but there must have been a considerable period during which people habitually *wrote* Latin naturally and thought they were still *speaking* it, a transitional period. During this it never seemed to occur to anyone to alter the liturgical language. For some time they must have thought it was the vernacular, and its ceasing to be so must have been very gradual. It was probably a long time before people realized that they were not talking Latin'. From a letter of Dr Henry Jenner, printed in *Orate Fratres* (St John's Abbey, Minn.), vol. 25, 1951, p. 84. Ireland no doubt received a Latin liturgy brought by St Patrick from Gaul. The languages of the English and the Germans at the time of their evangelization were doubtless considered too fluid and uncultivated to be used for liturgical purposes, if anybody ever thought of doing so. The attention of the reader may be drawn to Canon G. Bardy's *La question des langues dans l'Église ancienne* (Paris, 1948); and to the article 'Lingua liturgica', by Father J. M. Hanssens, in the new Italian *Enciclopedia Cattolica*, vol. vii.—*Trans.*]

3. [The rites of the Catholic Maronites and of the Catholic Malabarese are forms of the Antiochene and Chaldean rites respectively. For particulars of these rites and the churches that use them, see D. Attwater, *The Christian Churches of the East* (Milwaukee, 1948. 2 vols), and *Eastern Catholic Worship* (New York, 1945); A. A. King, *The Rites of Eastern Christendom* (Rome, 1947. 2 vols.).—*Trans.*]

4. [For these Western rites and uses see F. Cabrol, *The Mass of*

the Western Rites (London, 1934); R. C. West, *Western Liturgies* (London, *c.* 1939); A. A. King, *Liturgies of the Religious Orders* (London, 1954), and *Liturgies of the Primatial Sees* (London, 1957). —*Trans.*]

5. [Byelorussian is a preferable name to White Russian, as in English this last term is commonly used in another sense. In America the name Ruthenian is generally confined to people of Ukrainian origin who emigrated from elsewhere than Galicia (Halych) and Russian Ukraine.—*Trans.*]

6. [Historically the native Byzantine Christians of Syria, Palestine and Egypt are all Melkites, but nowadays there is a tendency to confine the name to the Catholics among them. In French they are often called 'Greeks', through a misunderstanding of the Turkish name Rûm, which signifies Roman, *i.e.* a former subject of New Rome (Constantinople). In Palestine and Egypt there are certain Orthodox churches whose congregations are properly Greek in nationality and therefore in liturgical language. —*Trans.*]

7. See the anonymous Nestorian history, later than the ninth century, in *Patrologia orientalis*, vol. vii, p. 117.

8. F. Nau, 'L'expansion nestorienne en Asie', in *Annales du Musée Guimet Bibliothèque du vulgarisation*, vol. xi (Paris, 1914), p. 252 note.

9. *The Mongol Mission*, ed. C. Dawson (London, 1955), pp. 137, 144.

10. Originally a katholikos was a bishop delegated by a patriarch to administer a distant region; these katholikoi gradually became independent hierarchs, but the title has persisted in Eastern canonical terminology. Among the Armenians, the katholikos, who was originally subject to the archbishop of Caesarea in Cappadocia, eventually fixed his see at Eshmiadzin in Transcaucasia and is now the supreme head of the dissident Armenian Church, above their patriarchs at Constantinople and Jerusalem; they have as well a lesser katholikate in Syria. Other dissident hierarchs also bear the title. Among Catholics, the Chaldean patriarch, who is historically the legitimate successor of the former hierarchs of Seleucia-Ctesiphon, has the title of katholikos, too; so does the Catholic Armenian patriarch, in virtue of his succession in the line of katholikoi of Sis and Cilicia.

11. The use of this expression shows that the writer was not a

Nestorian. Elsewhere it is made quite plain that he was a zealous monophysite.

12. A. Mingana, 'The Early Spread of Christianity in Central Asia and the Far East', in the *Bulletin of the John Rylands Library*, vol. ix (Manchester, 1925, p. 363). Also published separately.

13. See Migne, P. G., vol. cxxxviii, c. 957.

14. [The name Rumanian means Roman, and is more properly spelt Romanian.—*Trans.*]

15. He was bishop of Remesiana, which has been identified with Bela-Palanka, near Nish, in modern Serbia.

16. See M. Roques, *Palia d'Orastie*, vol. i (the only one published; Paris, 1925), pp. vii ff. The Palia is a Rumanian version of Genesis and Exodus, made by Protestants and published at Orastie in 1581–82.

17. At the beginning of the present century in Bukovina, Cyrillic was still used for the printing of some church books.

18. [J. S. Assemani (d. 1768), who was papal legate to the synod, was himself a Maronite and a very learned orientalist. Three other members of his family helped to make the name of Assemani famous among scholars.—*Trans.*] For the matters referred to, see pt. II, ch. xiii, no. 11, of the synodical acts, in *Collectio Lacensis*, vol. ii, c. 216.

19. See ch. iii, art. 2, of the acts of the synod; pp. 35–36 in the Roman edition (1896).

20. See sect. II, art. ii, no. 3, of the synodical acts; p. 52 of the Roman edition (1899).

21. In the review *Proche-Orient Chrétien* (St Ann's Seminary, Jerusalem) a very detailed study of this point has been made by Father Gabriel Giambernardini, O.F.M.: 'La réitération du Baptême chez les Coptes qui reviennent à l'unité', in vol. ii (1952), pp. 214–242, and vol. iii (1953), pp. 119–144, 306–322. It is substantially a question of the alteration of a Coptic word which completely changes the sense of the form. There are other examples in the *Collectanea* of the Congregation for the Spreading of the Faith. The most characteristic is in vol. ii, p. 9 (1907 edition), a decision of the Holy Office concerning eleven alterations in the form of baptism used among those Japanese Christians, discovered in 1865, who had kept their faith and its essential practices for two centuries though deprived of clergy. This decision of the Holy Office is a striking example of the utility of living language in

liturgy. The early Spanish missionaries had taught their catechists to baptize in Latin; but the Japanese have the greatest difficulty in pronouncing certain Latin letters and sounds (e.g., *f, tri, pti, spi*), and deformations inevitably followed. The same difficulty is experienced by the Chinese and other peoples of the Far East.

22. Nos. 629–633; pp. 304–305 in the Roman edition (1913).

23. This would hardly seem required in the Armenian rite since there is such a benediction towards the end of the eucharistic Liturgy, before communion.

Chapter Two

1. My documentation is based on numerous personal observations and communications, and on the chief publications of both sides: J. Szabo, *A Gorog-katholikus Magyarszag utolso kalvària-utja 1896–1912* ('The Way of Calvary followed by the Greek Catholics of Hungary from 1896 to 1912'; Budapest, 1913); *Schematismus Hajdorogensis ad* A.D. 1918 (Nyiregyhaza, 1919); *Libellus memorialis hungarorum graeci ritus catholicorum ad . . . Leonem XIII* (Budapest, 1900); I. Georgescu, *George Pop de Basesti* (Oradea Mare, 1935), a biography of one of the greatest Rumanian opponents of magyarization; *Emlelekkonyv a gorog szertartàsu katholikus Romai zaràndoklatàrol* ('Souvenir of the Pilgrimage to Rome of the Hungarian Catholics of Greek Rite'; Budapest, 1901); liturgical books in Hungarian, and Rumanian periodicals.

2. [In Eastern canonical terminology a diocese is called an eparchy. I translate this word as diocese in order not to confuse the Western reader.—*Trans.*]

3. [There are three forms of Mass liturgy in the Byzantine rite, viz., of St John Chrysostom, of St Basil and of St Gregory ('of the Presanctified'). The first is by far the most commonly used.—*Trans.*]

4. [At this battle in Bohemia the Prussians inflicted a decisive defeat on the Austrians.—*Trans.*]

5. The Austro-Hungarian administration called Slav and Rumanian Catholics of Byzantine rite 'Catholic Greeks'; dis-

sident Byzantines were called 'Eastern Greeks', the term Orthodox not being used officially.

6. [The eucharistic celebration, what is called The Mass in the West, is commonly referred to as The Liturgy in the Byzantine rite.—*Trans.*]

7. [It is normal among Eastern Christians, whether Catholic or dissident, that already married men are free to be ordained to the pastoral priesthood.—*Trans.*]

8. [Magyar=Hungarian (person and language).—*Trans.*]

9. [This does not mean that no responsible person had ever questioned the desirability of the exclusive use of Latin. See, for example, the views of the first United States bishop, discussed by Dr J. T. Ellis, 'Archbishop Carroll and the Liturgy in the Vernacular', in *Worship* (St John's Abbey, Minn.), vol. xxvi (1952), pp. 545–552.—*Trans.*]

10. By sheer chance this map came to rest in the Vatican Library, where I found it in 1925 among a batch of maps that came from the secretariate of state. Lest it be lost, I gave it the entry-number 42, 624, and the classified-number *Raccolta generale*, Carta I, 1. This material is not yet put in order and catalogued, but I am assured the map is still there.

11. Rumania proper had no representative at the Vatican, and there was no papal nuncio at Bucarest.

12. He was murdered by the Iron Guard in 1940.

13. The *Hieratikon*, or *Leitourgikon*, contains what is principally necessary for the celebrant at divine worship, and is a somewhat variable compilation.

14. [Blaj is the residence and administrative centre of the Catholic Rumanian metropolitan see of Fagaras and Alba Julia in Transylvania.—*Trans.*]

15. [Established by Pope Benedict XV in 1917.—*Trans.*]

16. [For a very interesting account of this, see 'The Podcarpathian Schism', by Father Vassily (Charles Bourgeois, S.J.), in *Pax*, nos. 147, 150 (Prinknash Abbey, 1934).—*Trans.*]

17. [In the official *Statistica . . . di rito orientale* (Rome, 1932) the number of Catholics in the diocese of Hajdudorog was given as 142,000.—*Trans.*]

18. I venture to refer readers who are interested in the subject to my articles in *Proche-Orient Chrétien* for the years 1953 and 1954. In them I outline a project for an Anthology, a logical and rational

abridgement of the twenty or so books that contain the Byzantine
Office, of which a considerable part is wholly monastic, or super-
fluous, or not in actual use.

Chapter Three

1. For what follows, particulars and full bibliography can be
found in A. Palmieri's excellent work, *La Chiesa russa . . .* (Florence,
1908), pp. 364-368, 484, 490, 505, 513, 515, 523; or in K. Lubeck,
Die russischen Missionen (Aachen, 1922). These are the only works
by Catholics that give a synthetic account of the missions of the
Russian Church. It is a pity they have not been translated into
English or French; but it is too late now, for the situation they
describe has been completely changed by the revolution. [There
is a useful little book by an Orthodox writer, S. Bolshakov,
Foreign Missions of the Russian Orthodox Church (London, 1943);
and see an article by N. Gorodetzky in *Eastern Churches Quarterly*
(St Augustine's Abbey, Ramsgate), vol. v (1943), pp. 117–129.—
Trans.]

2. The cultus of St Stephen of Perm is recognized by the
Catholic Church. [For him, see *Butler's Lives of the Saints* (London,
1956), vol. ii, p. 167. Perm is now called Molotov.—*Trans.*]

3. Though there are small differences of pronunciation in their
Arabic, a Syrian has no difficulty in understanding an Egyptian;
but the common Arabic of Lybia, Tunisia, Algeria and especially
Morocco is quite another matter: it is difficult for a Syrian to
understand a Moroccan and vice-versa. Yet the literary language
of all these countries is the same; but it is only written, or spoken
in formal speeches. Seventy years ago the Jesuits at the University
of Beirut published a magnificent Arabic Bible, carefully revised
by the best Christian Arabist of the time, Ibrahim Yazigi. From
this a volume containing the four gospels was extracted, for the
use of all rites that employ Arabic. But it was not a success, precisely because of its lexicographical and grammatical perfection:
people preferred the old versions, less correct but more easily
understood. A similar mishap befell the Catholic Melkites only

in 1953. A new edition of the *Horologion* was published and made
obligatory. The text had been drastically revised to bring it into
accordance with the pure style of the Qur'an, the great classic of
Arabic literature. But it was found that neither clergy nor people
could follow familiar passages or adapt them to the chant, so the
work has to be done again at a less exacting level. Hence a great
deal of confusion.

4. These French Orthodox number about seven hundred in the
whole of France. Some of them are people who have had difficulties of one sort or another with Catholic ecclesiastical authority;
others are attracted by services wholly in the language they understand: in my opinion these last are the more numerous. French
was already used in 1862–*c.* 1886 by another former Catholic, A. F.
Guettée, who had been led to the Russian Orthodox by his
'Gallican' views; he knew neither Russian nor Staroslav.

5. [Since he returned to America in 1932 to take charge of the
Orthodox Albanians there, Kyr Fan Noli has published further
books in Albanian, and prayer and hymn books in English. They,
too, are highly spoken of.—*Trans.*]

6. [Both among Orthodox and Catholics of Eastern rite in the
United States there is a desire for liturgy in English, varying in
degree of intensity according to factors operative in different
groups, and in some of the churches of both communions varying
amounts of English can already be heard at public worship, regularly or on certain occasions. The permission recently accorded
several times to an American bishop (of Roman rite) to celebrate
the Byzantine Mass almost wholly in English on special occasions
has undoubtedly made a most deep impression on those present,
not only Eastern Catholics but those of the Western rite as well.
—*Trans.*]

7. In view of the importance of all this, I give the original texts:

DUBBI.—(I) Se e come convenga permettere l'uso della lingua
estone nella celebrazione della santa Liturgia ai sacerdoti estoni di
rito bizantino. (2) Quali provvedimenti convenga adottare per il
caso del Rev. V. . . .

RESCRITTO.—Ad (1), Dilata, et ad mentem. Mens est, che si
puo fare sperare ai sacerdoti di rito bizantino l'uso della lingua

estone nella celebrazione della santa Liturgia. Intanto si faccia un diligente esame dei libri liturgici, per accertarsi se vi sia una versione presentabile espurgata da ogni errore. So potrà tuttavia concedere che nei tratti non segreti della santa Liturgia il popolo canti e risponda anche al celebrante nella propria lingua. Ad (2), [che il V . . . celebri nella versione esistente, dopo espurgazione].

Ex AUDIENTIA SS.MI., diei 20 februarii 1929.—Adprobantur (1) et (2), ad mentem. Mens est, il primo punto *non* si deve intendere come una restrizione di massima alla facoltà degli Orientali di usare le lingue più opportune al miglior bene delle anime nella liturgia, se la Santa Sede ne approva l'uso. Il secondo punto s'intende come una concessione per viam facti della lingua estone, che potrà essere applicata come precedente in casi simili.

8. [See an excellent little book by Father Charles Bourgeois, S.J., *A Priest in Russia and the Baltic* (London, 1953).—*Trans.*]

9. On 17 September, 1939, during the German onslaught on Poland, Galicia (Halych) and Byelorussia were occupied by the Russian army. This lasted for nearly two years, till the Germans took Lvov (Lviv) on 15 July, 1941. They were driven out by the Russians at the end of 1944, and this second occupation became definitive. Metropolitan Szepticky died soon after; work on the cause of his beatification has been begun.

10. [They appear possibly to belong to the Uralian family.—*Trans.*]

11. See Migne, P. G., vol. xlix, c. 188. On the whole question, see C. Charon, 'L'origine ethnographique des Melkites' in *Échos d'Orient*, vol. xi (1908), pp. 35-40, 82-91.

12. [A point arising out of Eastern canon law has here led the learned author rather far afield. The passage and its long footnote are therefore omitted.—*Trans.*]

13. A *troparion* is a hymnodic strophe; a combination of *troparia* forms a *kanon*, more or less long; *stikhera* are *troparia* inserted between the verses of psalms. Greek liturgical poetry, the work of men who were both poets and musicians, is not based upon the metres of classical poetry and the quantity of syllables, but on their number and the tonic accent, something like the Latin rhythmic proses of the middle ages.

14. See, for example, in the *Menaion* for December, the second

kanon of Christmas Matins; for January, the second *kanon* of the Epiphant; and, in the *Pentekostarion*, the second *kanon* of Whitsunday. In practice, they are rarely sung in the offices.

15. On these translations, see two articles by T. Xanthopoulos in *Échos d'Orient*, vol. v. (1902), pp. 321–332, and vol. vi (1903), pp. 230–240. At the end of the second article there is a specimen of modern Greek as it is spoken. [In 1956 a decree of the Ministry of Worship and Education in Athens forbade the use in schools of these translations published by foreign Bible societies. An official version of the New Testament in the modern tongue seems to be in preparation.—*Trans.*]

16. *L'Empire des tsars et les russes* (Paris, 1898), vol. iii, p. 86. This third volume is still worth reading; the first two, especially the second, are quite out of date.

17. [Tigrinya is a language, Tigré is both a language and a social caste, Tigrai is a region. These names are variously spelt in European languages, and much confusion results.—*Trans.*]

18. [*Negus negesti*, 'king of kings" commonly referred to as 'emperor' in English.—*Trans.*]

19. [This seems especially true in North America. For example, *Christ with us*, an excellent pocket Mass-book, and *We Magnify Thee*, a short book of occasional services, both of Catholic Ukrainian origin (Stamford, Conn., 1954); or the very handy Catholic Rumanian *Manual of Prayers and Services* (Cleveland, Ohio, 1946). —*Trans.*]

20. [We are now seeing its beginnings, in those places that have been accorded a partly vernacular Ritual.—*Trans.*]

21. Except in the new arrangement called biritualism, when he can do as he judges best.

22. [Nevertheless, the liberal spirit of the East continues to operate. The translator has been present at a Chaldean Liturgy in England when the epistle was read in English only by a lector.]

23. [Excellent examples are the services for Benediction devised for the Greek Catholic colony in Corsica and for the Melkites, in Greek and Arabic respectively. See *Orate Fratres* (St John's Abbey, Minn.), vol. xii, pp. 490–495.—*Trans.*]

M

PART II

Chapter One

1. *Glagol* means speech, word; it is also the name of the fourth letter of the Slavonic alphabet, corresponding to *g*.

2. [It is possible that St Clement I died in exile in those parts, but extremely unlikely that the relics brought to Rome by St Cyril and St Methodius in 867 were really his.—*Trans.*]

3. [*Liber sacramentorum romanae ecclesiae:* Capitular Library of Padua, codex D.47. See p. 23 of Father Sakač's article referred to in the next note.—*Trans.*]

4. For the essential data of this very complex question, see A. Raes, *Introductio ad liturgiam orientalem* (Rome, 1947), pp. 223–224; and for a full account of it, S. Sakač's 'SS. Cyril and Methodius and the Origin of the Romano-Slavic Rite' in *Unitas*, vol. i, no. 2 (Rome, 1949), pp. 22–29. [For St Methodius's translation of the contemporary Roman rite, see pp. 27–29 of this article; and for the Liturgy of St Peter see the work of that name by H. W. Codrington and P. de Meester (Münster, 1936).—*Trans.*]

5. [Sometimes called Stephen VI, according to whether Stephen II, who died on the third day after his election in 752, is counted or not.—*Trans.*]

6. Formosus later became pope, from 891 to 896. [He seems to have been a man of good personal life, but weak in character and judgement.—*Trans.*]

7. [A *regesta* is a collection of official copies of papal letters and other documents kept in the pontifical archives.—*Trans.*]

8. For the detailed demonstration of all this, see A. Lapôtre, *Le pape Jean VIII* (Paris, 1895), notably pp. 3–29, for the history of the *regesta*, and pp. 123–170 (especially 133–135), for the proofs of Wiching's forgery. I have simply summarized this excellent work for this period of the religious history of the Slavs in the West.

9. '*Nec sanae fidei vel doctrinae aliquid obstat sive missas in eadem sclavinica lingua canere, sive sacrum Evangelium vel lectiones divinas*

Novi et Veteris Testamenti bene translatas et interpretatas legere, aut alia horarum officia psallere' (Migne, P. L., vol. cxxvi, col. 906).

10. See Migne, P. L., vol. clxviii, col. 557.

11. This is stated by A. d'Avril in 'Le glagol et la Congregation des Rites', in *Revue de l'Orient chrétien*, vol. iv (1899), pp. 3–4.

12. Urban VIII's bull approving the Slavonic Missal, *'Ecclesia catholica'*, is dated 29 April, 1631; Innocent X's for the Breviary, *'Romanum Pontificem'*, 22 February, 1648; the Yugoslav concordat, 25 July, 1935.—Other bibliographical particulars can be found in N. Nilles, *Kalendarium manuale utriusque ecclesiae . . .*, 2nd edn. (Innsbrück, 1896), pp. 502–507; and in A. d'Avril, *art. cit.*, note 11 above, pp. 5–13. Cf. the *Collectanea* of the Congregation for the Spreading of the Faith, 2nd edn. (Rome, 1907), vol. i, p. 74, no. 220; vol. ii, p. 271, no. 1785.—The Missal of 1631 was revised by a Croat, the Franciscan Raphael Levaković; after editions in 1706 and 1731, a new one was supervised by Archbishop Matthew Caraman of Zadar in 1741. About 1890 a further revision was entrusted to a Ruthenian, who introduced a good number of usages from his own tongue. The edition had to be destroyed, and it was then that Dr Vajs was called on. His translation is philologically very correct: his language is the real Staroslav, without the slight orthographical and morphological modifications found in the modern Slav-Byzantine liturgical books. The biblical passages follow the Vulgate rigorously. This edition is called *Rimski Misal slovenskim jezikom*, 'The Roman Missal in the Slavonic Language', and only the canon is printed in Glagolitic as well as Roman characters.

13. [According to the *Catholic Encyclopaedia*, vol. xv, p. 369, Father Kassić had made an Illyrian version of the Bible in 1632. —*Trans.*]

14. *Zbirka svetih obredov za lavantinsko in ljubljansko skofijo.* The diocese of Lavant is also known as Maribor.

15. *Rituale in usum cleri regularis et saecularis totius Bosniae et Hercegovinae, iussu et auctoritate Josephi Stadler metropolitae et archiepiscopi Vrhbonensis . . . editum.*

Chapter Two

1. The letter is dated 8 January, 1305: the text is in the *Journal of the Royal Asiatic Society*, 1914, p. 551; translation of the second and third letters in *The Mongol Mission*, ed. C. Dawson (London, 1955), pp. 224–227. John of Monte Corvino was appointed archbishop of Khanbalik (Peking) in 1307. [Cf. Raynaldus, *Annales ecclesiastici*, ad ann. 1305, xix–xx, and 1307, xxix–xxx.]

2. See *Bullarium Ordinis Fratrum Praedicatorum*, vol. ii (Rome, 1730), p. 370; *Collectio Lacensis*, vol. ii, col. 538.

3. The original text of the rescript is lost, but there is a later abstract of it; this was examined in *Stoudion*, vol. v (Rome, 1928), pp. 65–69, by Mgr. Angelo Mercati, prefect of the Vatican Archives. The same article contains details of the case of Manuel Chrysoloras.

4. See F. Tournebize, 'Les Frères Uniteurs . . . ou Dominicains arméniens', in *Revue de l'Orient chrétien*, vol. xxii (1920–21), pp. 145–161 and 249–279. There are other writings on the subject. [Cf. M. A. van der Oudenrijn, *Annotationes bibliographicae Armeno-Dominicanae* (Rome, 1921), pp. 42–47.]

5. Quétif and Echard, *Scriptores O.P.* (Paris, 1719), vol. i, p. 582.

6. That at any rate was the opinion of the abbot general of the Mekhitarist monks at Venice, Sukias Somal: see his *Quadro della storia litteraria di Armenia* (Venice, 1829), p. 170.

7. 'La discipline de l'Église en matière de langue liturgique', in *Langues et traductions liturgiques*, No. 11 of *La Maison-Dieu* (Paris, 1947).

8. For what follows, see *Concilium Tridentinum*, vol. v (Freiburg i. B., 1919), pp. 742, 753, 757, 766, 771, 780, 911 (ch. 8), 912–915, 962–965.

9. [Canon Martimort remarks drily that nobody seems to have been impressed by the 'three languages' argument. On the other hand, Santis emphasized that the Pope could alter the discipline on this point if he thought fit.—*Trans.*]

10. [This bishop was Thomas Goldwell, who lived to be the last survivor of the old episcopate of England and Wales. He was the only English bishop at the Council of Trent. He did not think the reasons for rejecting the vernacular were of sufficient weight. —*Trans.*]

11. Attention must be drawn to the very important monograph

by Father Herman Schmidt, *Liturgie et langue vulgaire* (Analecta Gregoriana, vol. liii, Rome, 1950), which examines the question among the early Reformers and at the Council of Trent. Father Schmidt, however, recalls Ferrand's statement without noticing the mistake that had been made, writing of 'The text of Justinian's *Novellae Constitutiones*, where we read that bishops and priests should celebrate the liturgy in the language of the people. . . .'

12. *Op. cit.*, note 11, p. 134.

13. [In the encyclical letter 'Mediator' (1947), Pope Pius XII writes: 'The use of the Latin language prevailing in a great part of the Church affords both an imposing sign of unity and an effective safeguard against the corruption of doctrine. Admittedly the adoption of the vernacular in quite a number of services may prove of great benefit to the faithful. But to make such concessions is for the Apostolic See alone. . . .' Since those words were written, the Apostolic See has formally recognized an element of spoken languages in the worship of the whole Western church: during the vigil service on Easter night, for the renewal of baptismal promises and the common saying of the Lord's Prayer with which this ends.— *Trans.*]

14. Archives of Propaganda, *Acta*, vol. vii (1630–31), fos. 54–55.

15. The relevant rescript may be found in a work that is very difficult to get hold of, because the second volume was not printed and the whole edition was dispersed when the Propaganda Press was brought to an end under Pope St Pius X: it is R. de Martinis, *Ius pontificium de Propaganda Fide*, pt 2, *Decreta* (Rome, 1899), p. 18, no. 14. The editor has confused Arabic with Persian, probably reproducing a mistake of the original, but the true meaning is clear. In an article in *Neue Zeitschrift für Missionswissenschaft* (Beckenried, Switzerland), p. 244, Father Nicholas Kowalsky points out that it was a question of the literary and not the spoken language, and that the Congregation thus did not contradict the decree of Trent which speaks of the vernacular. [See A. V. Seumois, *La papauté et les missions au cours des six premiers siècles* (Paris, 1953), pp. 165–166.— *Trans.*]

16. See R. de Martinis, previous note, p. 32, no. 46; or the Propaganda *Collectanea* (1907), vol. i, p. 11, no. 33.

17. Archives of Propaganda, *Acta* for 1757, fo. 519.

18. Propaganda, *Lettere della Sacra Congregazione* for 1777, fo. 81

19. *Acta* for 1784, fos. 487, 520.

20. *Acta* for 1824, fo. 147; *Collectanea*, vol. i, no. 782; *Acta* for 1827, fo. 467; L. Lemmens *Acta S. Cong. de Prop. Fide pro Terra Sancta*, pt. ii (Quaracchi, 1922), p. 72.

21. *Op. cit.*, note 7 above, pp. 52–53. Canon Martimort gives a reference to Delplace, *Synopsis actorum*, p. 271, nos. 162, 164; I have not been able to consult this collection.

22. There are two copies of this Missal in the Vatican Library (*Borgiani cinesi* 352, 409), where they have been left among the manuscripts in order not to disarrange an established section.

23. *Collectanea*, vol. ii, p. 234, no. 394.

24. [In the course of a report supporting his application Father Couplet wrote: 'I may be allowed to ask whether, had the leaders of the Apostles, Peter and Paul, come to preach in China, would they not have done what they did in Rome and Athens, where they put aside Aramaic because Latin and Greek were there the languages? Would they not in China have used Chinese for divine worship?' (Quoted by Martimort, *op. cit.*, p. 53, from *Acta Sanctorum, Propylaeum Maji*, Paralipomena).—*Trans.*]

25. Propaganda archives: Special committees for the Indies and China, 1755–56, fo. 65; Letters for the East Indies, 1755–59, fos. 39, 308–9; Special committees, 1770–73, fo. 320. *Collectanea*, vol. i, nos. 422, 500 (where 'September' should read 'December').

26. [The old-established 'German high Mass', as it is often called, was authoritatively regularized in 1943 for Germany, Austria, Luxemburg and parts of Switzerland. It provides for the choral parts of the ordinary to be sung by the people at *Missa cantata* in a free translation in German.—It appears that Pope Pius XII has assured Cardinal Tien, archbishop of Peking, that in due course Mandarin Chinese will be accorded for the liturgy in China, the canon of the Mass alone being retained in Latin: cf. S. Paventi, *La Chiesa missionaria* (Rome, 1949), p. 388. A Chinese altar Missal has already been printed in China.—*Trans.*]

27. Perhaps I may be allowed to clear up a peculiar point here. The concordat referred to was in Italian, but in the official edition of the Acts of Leo XIII it carries the Latin title of *Conventio inter Sanctam Sedem et Principem amaniensem*. Why, one may ask, did the editor not say simply *Montis Nigri*, which is certainly Latin? He was a bit of a humanist and did not find that expression classical enough; but he did find that in the Cilician Taurus there is a range of peaks that in antiquity were called *Amanus*, now Kara-Dagh,

Black Mountain, in Turkish. The fact that the Taurus is in Asia Minor and Montenegro is in Europe does not seem to have worried him.

28. [A remarkable example from the New World seems to have escaped the learned author. It was thus described, in a letter to the translator in 1951, by Father Yvan Forest, S.J., of Montreal: 'The Iroquois Indians have the privilege of singing their part of high Mass in Iroquois, not only on feasts but every time they wish. But of the origin of that privilege there is no trace anywhere. And nobody can state any date of the origin of it. Even the oldest priests used to refer to it as an 'immemorial tradition' of the old days. The singing comprises both the proper and the common. The Iroquois in low Masses (usually the Sisters with the children) use dialogue Mass or prayers in common, not in Iroquois (the children know it very little) but in English.' Concessions have now been made to certain mission territories for vernacular singing by the people (*Kyrie, Gloria*, etc.) at sung Mass. And in France permission has recently (1956) been given for the epistle and gospel at every Mass to be repeated in French *immediately* after each has been read or sung in Latin.—*Trans.*]

29. The translator was one Joseph de Voisin. There must have been a previous attempt, to account for the faculty of theology's censure in 1655. The first complete edition of Voisin's *Le Missel romain, selon le règlement du Concile de Trente* appeared in four volumes in Paris in 1660; the second, in six volumes, in 1668. The convocation of French clergy declared excommunication against whoever should read this work on 7 December, 1660; Alexander VII issued his brief of prohibition, '*Ad aures nostras*" on 12 January, 1661.

30. [There are many other examples, and earlier ones. In Canada, for instance, there was a French-Latin *Missel et Vespéral* giving the canon of the Mass integrally in French at least as early as 1908. The first English-Latin Missal with *complete* English and Latin texts was published by Desclée in 1910; the unnamed editor and translator of this was the late Abbot Thomas Bergh, monk of Ramsgate, but this was not the first time that the whole of the *canon* had been given in English. I am indebted to Dom Paulinus Ievers for the contents of this note.—*Trans.*]

31. The *motu proprio* is here simply repeating a decree of the Congregation of Rites of 22 May, 1894 (*Decreta authentica*, no. 3827).

32. [In the German book these words, 'Ego conjungo vos . . . ,' are omitted altogether, their place being taken by a ratification and blessing by the priest in the name of the Church, followed by a call to the congregation as witnesses. In the American book, the Latin words are retained, but followed by these in English: 'I call upon all of you here present to be witnesses of this holy union which I have now blessed. "What God has joined together let no man put asunder".'—*Trans.*]

PART III

Chapter One

1. For all the first part of this exceedingly complicated story of the Malabar Church and its liturgical books I hardly do more than summarize Cardinal Tisserant's exhaustive article, 'Syro-malabare (Église)' in the *Dictionnaire de théologie catholique*, vol. xiv (1941), cc. 3089–3162.

2. [*Mar*, equivalent to *dominus*, is the title of bishops in Syrian churches. It is also used for saints; feminine, *mart.—Trans.*]

3. For this title and office, see note 10 to the first chapter of Part I. The official title of the Catholic katholikos at Mosul is now Patriarch of Babylon of the Chaldeans, from an erroneous identification of modern Baghdad with ancient Babylon.

4. A. de Gouvea, *Jornada de Arcebispo de Goa dom Frey Aleixo de Menezes* . . . (Coïmbra, 1606). The book is very rare. There is a French version of a Spanish translation: J. B. de Glen, *Histoire orientale des grands progrès de l'Église catholique* (Brussels and Antwerp, 1609).

5. The *padroado* (Port., patronage) was the privilege whereby the sovereigns of Portugal had the right to present persons to the Holy See to fill bishoprics established in regions opened up by Portuguese venturers.

6. [Dr J. C. Panjikaran, in *Christianity in Malabar*, no. 23 of *Orientalia Christiana* (Rome, 1926), p. 123, and other writers, give a somewhat different account of the establishment of the Jacobite hierarchy in Malabar. See L. W. Brown, *The Indian Christians of St Thomas* (Cambridge, 1956), ch. v.—*Trans.*]

7. Cf. the third section of Part I, Chapter Three.

8. [Palliveetil Shandy remained bishop of his people for fourteen years, till his death in 1687. He did much to undo the divisive work of his cousin.—*Trans.*]

9. Cf. the third section of Part I, Chapter Three.

10. *L'Uniatisme: Définition, causes, effets, étendue, dangers, remèdes* (Irénikon-Collection, nos. 5–6; Prieuré d'Amay, Belgium, 1927), p. 46.

Chapter Two

1. Cf. Part I, the fourth section of Chapter One and the fourth section of Chapter Three.

2. The whole confused story is related, but not very clearly, by M. Chaine in *Revue de l'Orient chrétien*, vol. xiv (1909), pp. 321–329; there is a better account, by I. Ortiz de Urbina, in *Dictionnaire d'histoire et de géographie ecclésiastiques*, vol. viii (Paris, 1935), cc. 542–543.

3. [Before him, other priests had given their lives in attempting to penetrate the country, among them the two French Capuchins, Agathangelo and Cassian, who were beatified in 1905.—*Trans.*]

4. [This great man was beatified in 1939, thirteen years after his helper, the martyred Gabra Mika'el.—*Trans.*]

5. [These words irresistably call to mind the very different sentiments of Pope Pius XI when founding the Oriental Institute at Rome in 1928; he spoke of 'being moved to a yet warmer love for the true Bride of Christ' by looking upon her 'entrancing beauty in the diversity of her various rites'.—*Trans.*]

6. The provision was made in the brief '*Apostolatus officium*' of 6 July, 1847, naming Justin de Jacobis titular bishop of Nilopolis and vicar apostolic of Abyssinia. This brief is missing from vol. vi of the *Juris pontificii de propaganda fide* of R. de Martinis (Rome, 1894). The same faculty is mentioned in a letter, also unpublished, of Pius IX to Ras Haylu, 'Lieutenant of the Emperor of Abyssinia', in 1850. The privilege was extended to all the Vincentians in Ethiopia in the same year, and it seems also to the first successors of de Jacobis until Mgr Touvier (1870–88); cf. Metodio of Nembro, *La missione dei Minori Cappuccini in Eritrea* (Rome, 1953), pp. 363–364 and notes. This work, very conscientiously carried out from the archives of the mission, includes a chapter called *Rito etiopico* wherein the facts are exact, barring a very few small points. The

author does not take sides with either the latinizers or the eastern-izers. I complete it from personal observations, having been closely concerned with the whole question since 1930. Now that at least the essential texts are available, the Eastern Congregation grants the privilege of biritualism to all who ask for it, provided they are properly qualified.

7. [Eritrea is the coastal region of Ethiopia which was an Italian colony from 1885 till 1941. Ethiopia and Abyssinia are alternative names for the whole country; Ethiopia is more correct.—*Trans.*]

8. See Metodio of Nembro, *op. cit.*, note 6 above, pp. 373-377.

9. These supplements comprised the biblical canticles, hymns to the Mother of God (*Wedasê Maryam*), and the hour of Prime (*Ankatsa berkhân*: 'gate of the dawn'). The second edition (Asmara, 1931) added Matins (*Kidân za-naghê*), Vespers (*Kidân za-sarek*), prayers for divers objects, and the daily litany for the dead (*litôn*).

10. Father Metodio (*op. cit.*, p. 379), doubts the existence of a reply, and I have not found any trace of one either.

11. On his own authority, Father Coulbeaux added the words 'for us' to the epiklesis (' . . . that they may be made *for us* the body and blood . . .'), to bring it closer to the Roman formula. He himself told this to one of his colleagues at Rome, from whom I learned it. My informant had expressed surprise, and Father Coulbeaux replied, 'Who would notice it?' The commission referred to later on was quick to notice it, and deleted the inter-polated words.

12. See a good obituary notice, with bibliography, by E. Cerulli in *Oriente moderno*, vol. xxii (1942), pp. 516-517.

13. This was undeniable. The regulation is set out in so many words in Mgr. Carrara's book of rules, referred to previously, pp. 103-104.

14. [Some Catholic Easterners sing these words in the Creed, others do not. Their omission makes no difference to their belief in the pertinent doctrine.—*Trans.*]

15. [The pope himself is nominally the prefect of this con-gregation.—*Trans.*]

16. [A former see in North Africa. An ordinariate is a region in which the faithful of an Eastern rite are subject to a prelate, usually a titular bishop, of their rite who has ordinary powers and duties in respect of them; his jurisdiction is personal rather than

territorial. The hierarch and his jurisdiction are now called 'exarch' and 'exarchate'.—*Trans.*]

17. H. Denzinger, *Ritus orientalium . . . in administrandis sacramentis* (Würzburg, 1863–64, 2 vols). Johann Scholz (d. 1852), a Catholic priest, was professor of exegesis at the University of Bonn.

18. Vansleb or Wansleben, *Histoire de l'Église d'Alexandrie* (Paris, 1677). Vansleb ministered for a long time in Cairo, and knew the last recorded man who spoke Coptic naturally.

19. He published his *Institutiones liturgicae de ritibus orientalibus* in 1931–32 (Rome, 2 vols.).

20. See Metodio of Nembro, *op. cit.*, note 6 above, pp. 425–444.

CONCLUSION

1. [For a complete English translation of Cardinal Lercaro's address, and of other proceedings of the Congress, see *Worship*, vol. xxviii, no. 3 (St John's Abbey, Collegeville, Minn., 1954). On the whole subject with reference to England and the English language, see *English in the Liturgy: a Symposium*, edited by C. R. A. Cunliffe (London, 1956).—*Trans.*]

2. Anti-religious politics helped to bring this work to an end. See L. Baunard, *Le cardinal Lavigerie*, vol. i (Paris, 1896), pp. 199–227, 412–442. [For a short note, see D. Attwater, *The White Fathers in Africa* (London, 1937), pp. 9–11.]

3. [According to *Chambers's Encyclopaedia* (1950 edn.) there are about a hundred thousand Parsis in India.—*Trans.*]

4. [Cf. S. K. Dhalla, *Zoroastrianism* (1914); J. H. Moulton, *Treasure of the Magi* (1917); references in E. S. Drower, *Water into Wine* (1956); and J. Menant, *Les Parsis*, in Annales du Musée Guimet.—*Trans.*]

5. Meanwhile it is to be hoped that the Latin-rite bishops will cease to oppose Malabarese missionaries preaching the Gospel to the heathen outside their own ecclesiastical province unless they change their rite, which is the case hitherto. There is a fine field

of action here for the Malabarese Carmelite tertiary fathers and congregations of nuns.

6. So 'unforeign' was this church by the end of thirty years or so, that during the Russo-Japanese war of 1904–05 its bishop, though a Russian, was left unmolested.

INDEX